LUCAS ON LIFE

DEDICATION

To Kris and Andrew

Lucas on Life

JEFF LUCAS

AUTHENTIC PUBLISHING
Milton Keynes, England

LUCAS ON LIFE

Published 2001 by Word Publishing.
This reprint published by Authentic Publishing,
9 Holdom Avenue, Bletchley, Milton Keynes, Bucks, MK1 1QR, UK.

Reprinted 2001 (twice), 2002

ISBN: 1-86024-360-6

Cover design by David Lund

Book production for Authentic Publishing by
Bookprint Creative Services, P.O. Box 827, BN21 3YJ, England.
Printed in Great Britain.

CONTENTS

ACKNOWLEDGEMENTS

Life is about friendship – with God, with his people, and with those who have not yet bumped into him. I am so grateful to the friends with whom I am able to drink a toast to life. Chris and Jeanne, Ishmael and Irene, Dary and Bonnie, Ken and Debbie, Lindsay, Dinah and Stuart, Ben, Paul and Priscilla, Malc and Kathy, Ian and Andie, Dave and Pat, Adrian and Pauline, Dave and Sandra, and Stuart and Irene, are just a few who have enriched the journey so far . . .

My colleagues on the Spring Harvest Leadership Team have become trusted friends: Rachael, Ian, Gerard, Alan and the esteemed 'His Bishopness', Pete.

My thanks to the two churches of which I am now a part: Revelation Church, Chichester, and Timberline Church, Fort Collins, Colorado.

I'm grateful to the publishers of *Compass* and *Christianity & Renewal* magazines for allowing me to use material that has appeared on their pages, and to Kingsway Publications for permission to use some anecdotal material already published in *Gideon: Power from Weakness*, which I wrote in 1999.

And to my closest companions on the journey – Kay, Kelly and Richard – I love you.

INTRODUCTION

I fretted endlessly over the title, because I was terrified that you, dear reader, might think that I was suggesting that I was setting myself up as some kind of fountainhead of wisdom or self-professed expert. Nothing could be farther from the truth. I'm currently forty-four years of age (I look older, I've had a rough passage), and it won't take you many chapters of this book to work out that when it comes to living, I'm still in the nursery school. That's why this book is not a 'Seventy-seven Sure Pathways to Success' product with a picture of the serenely happy Lucas family grinning with cheesy delight on the back cover.

I am actually quite a gifted idiot. My profession of stupidity is not self-effacing. It's not pseudo-humility: it's for real. Find hope here – God uses idiots. He hasn't got anything else to choose from. Encouraging, eh?

Sometimes I think I exist just to provide hours of rib-tickling entertainment to my friends. Whoever hangs out with me becomes a witness to the seemingly never-ending stream of odd happenings and ridiculous events that seem to be birthed wherever I go. The sad thing (for me – my friends are delighted) is that most of the strange stuff that happens to me is because of my own ineptitude or lack of awareness . . .

Like today. I recently felt a major desire to be trendy, and so I dragged my elderly body into the 'Quicksilver' clothing store, and purchased a rather nice blue jacket. I wore it proudly later that day, and then, this morning, I decided to take a walk with

Kay and some friends: an ideal opportunity to don the aforesaid jacket. I put it on, and sought some affirmation and admiration from my less-trendy friends. 'What do you think? Nice, uh?'

They burst out laughing.

I had been strolling around blissfully unaware of the huge 'special reduction – won't last' label that was hanging from the back collar. Notice of the reduction was scrawled in huge back felt tip pen.

And so *Lucas on Life* is no collection of wisdom from one deeply profound; no deep musings from an inspiring and learned sage. Rather, I've drawn together a collection of stories and episodes that hopefully will make you laugh, sometimes make you cry, and occasionally make you think. I speak as someone who loves God, but messes up life constantly. I fall asleep when I pray and, occasionally, when I wake up in the morning I wonder if it's all real. I have been known to shout at my kids and say unkind words to my wife. I'm a Christian, but I'm not terribly good at it.

I freely admit that my view on life is blinkered. I've been in 'full-time' Christian leadership for the last twenty years, and so know little about the everyday pressures of strap-hanging on the London Underground (although I did that for a year while working for Barclays Bank); the pressures of short term working contracts; unemployment; and all kinds of other everyday pressures that constitute life in the third millennium. But I have known what it is to step out in faith, to have to trust God for the next penny or pound, and I have seen more than my fair share of divine interventions and incidents.

A very conservative evangelical newspaper recently reviewed one of my earlier books and branded me as a 'liberal Arminianist with mystical tendencies'. The publisher rushed me a copy of their review, a little nervous at their somewhat savage remarks. Analysing their comments carefully (because constructive criticism is the only way to growth), I worked out that they considered me to be 'Arminianist', because I happen to believe that there is an openness in the heart of God towards his people; that everything is not pre-ordained, eternally set in stone, fixed in advance. If it were, what would be the point in prayer? If history is all fixed ahead of time, but God gives us the impression that it isn't, to encourage us to pray, surely that is nothing less than divine deceit. I believe that prayer – and therefore we – can change things. This is exciting, and makes me want to nip behind the bike sheds for a crafty prayer . . .

I then worked out that they considered me to have 'mystical tendencies' because I believe that God speaks today through prophetic words: that the gifts of the Spirit were not on temporary loan. The pages that follow are peppered with accounts of prophesies and healing and, even though the saying has been over-used and indeed misused, you will hear me say 'God spoke to me' more than once. Lest there be any doubt, let me declare that I am rooted to the anchor of God's final authority being vested in the pages of Scripture. But my commitment to that Scripture will not allow me to edit out the reality that leaps from its pages – the reality of the supernatural God and his supernatural church. If I am 'mystical' because of this, then I'm happy to stand shoulder to shoulder with the growing millions across the earth whose lives have been touched and changed through some work, gift or manifestation of the Holy Spirit. I insist that you know that the dramatic, exciting episodes that you will read about have happened over a period of twenty-five years, lest you think that I and my family live a 'grinaholic, blessing-every-moment' existence. But they did – and do happen.

And what about the 'liberal' tag? I'm unsure about that, but wondered whether it might be because I believe in fun before death. I love laughter, and do not believe that joy is some subterranean flicker of happiness that is mined so deep within us that it would take a nuclear explosion to get it out.

I am nervous of that intense seriousness that masquerades as sobriety. I don't enjoy sermons that are so 'deep' that no one has the slightest idea what the preacher is on about. In short, I don't feel the need to become one of the 'frozen chosen'. I will talk freely – and, I hope, not offensively – about matters like sex, death and other things that we can tend to tiptoe around in the name of 'appropriateness'. You may not always agree with me, but I hope that you will hear my heart, and when in doubt, give me the benefit of the doubt.

Thanks for buying the book. And if you haven't bought it yet, and are standing reading this is in the local Christian bookshop, then buy it now. Pleeeease. . . .

Thank you.

Jeff Lucas
Chichester 2001

EVANGELISM

TRAIN MAN

He has no name, this man. I have him tagged in my mental filing cabinet under 'T' for 'Train Man'. We have met but twice.

My knowledge of *Homosapius Railtrack* is scant. His large frame ages him at somewhere between thirty and fifty and he lives somewhere in the Chichester area. He is red-faced and rotund, he is not gifted in the art of shaving, and he isn't at all on friendly terms with soap. He wears his belt askew and his flies very undone, even in the chill of winter. And he is a devotee of Transcendental Meditation in particular, and anything mildly 'New Agey' in general.

We first met a year ago. I had planned my railway journey with meticulous, even military, precision. My bag was over-stuffed with dog-eared papers, laptop computer, mobile phone, and other accessories of pressure. Determined to make the best use of time, I had even visited the 'Gentlemen's' prior to boarding the train, thus saving me time and exempting me from the need to hold my breath and fight my way into the putrid, toxic zone, otherwise known as the Connex South Central toilet.

I was feeling alive, efficient, and, quite frankly, fairly spiritually attuned. Only the night before, I had experienced a heavy 'double really' encounter with God, during which I had affirmed – I mean really, really affirmed – my desire to be more openly evangelistic in my personal life.

I opened the laptop lid and punched 'on'. And suddenly 'Train Man' climbed into my carriage, struggled to slam the door behind

him, and sat down opposite me, although there were many empty
seats. I stared intently at the computer screen, which was still blank.
The computer was still starting – he started immediately. 'Train
Man' is one of those people that the politically incorrect would
describe as 'simple'. By that, I mean that he apparently engages
everyone he meets in avid conversation, as if they were old
friends. How strange that, in our techno-lonely culture, a willing-
ness to socialise should be seen as a sign of poor mental health.

He started, unfazed by my staring obsession with the still
wretchedly blank screen. No 'Nice day isn't it/Makes a change to
see some sunshine/Is this the Victoria train?' prelude for him. He
plunged clumsily into my life with both huge feet.

'What are you doing?' he demanded, a warm smile softening
the abruptness of the question, with a sudden display of crooked,
yellow teeth.

'I'm writing an article about Christianity', I replied, feeling an
immediate rush of smugness that I had lined up with all of the
martyrs of the faith in my bold affirmation.

'You don't believe all that stuff, do you?' he shot back: no
nervous trepidation in his voice. The laptop told me that Windows
was made in 1995 and was now ready to receive my wisdom. With
one eye on the screen, and one eye on 'Train Man', I confirmed that
I did believe in the Jesus stuff and, with a deep breath, enquired as
to why he didn't. I didn't really want to know. I wanted to work.

And for the next twenty minutes, he told me about his
spirituality: about his feeling that Christians had no right to claim
exclusive rights to God. The laptop beeped and my mobile phone
rang twice, but he hardly paused for breath.

Worthing station came, and he went. But, after slamming the
door behind him, he came back to yell a few more of his jumbled
thoughts through the open window, loudly, but kindly, and then,
as the train inched and shuddered away, he stood and waved me
goodbye, like a farewell for an old friend.

I then forgot all about 'Train Man'. Until yesterday.

I had spoken on Sunday about evangelism. 'I am not ashamed

of the gospel' was the text from the first chapter of Romans. We smashed clay pots at the end of the talk, signifying our determination to 'let our light shine'. Symbolism is rich – and easy.

Monday morning found me on the London train, animatedly engaged in conversation with a professional lady – 'in publishing, actually' – who was bound for a business meeting in East Grinstead – 'East Grin, actually'. We talked back and forth about doing up houses and builders and living in lovely Chichester and the like. And then, the compartment door slid open, and in stepped 'Train Man', his belt positioned just below his nipples, and his open fly impossibly, hugely, gaping. He didn't recognise me, probably because of countless thousands of conversations since our first meeting, but he greeted me and the lady bound for Grin like old friends. Stealing a millisecond glance at the black hole in his trousers, the lady turned discreetly away. I said hello and stared hopefully at my shoes.

During the next twenty minutes, he informed me about his gallstones and the medication his doctor had given him and would I take Methadone? He showed me his brand new ivory yin/yang ring, surely worth a lot, but picked up for a mere fiver from a mate, which was amazing seeing as ivory was a precious metal, wasn't it?

'Elephant tusk', I said, and thought about mentioning his unemployed zipper.

The compartment filled with the musty, sour smell of an unwashed body. 'Grin' wrinkled her nose and scowled her disapproval; 'Train Man' talked on; I urged the train on towards Worthing with a prayerful whip. 'Train Man' looked into my eyes, and his own quizzical, smiling eyes seeming to reach down into my soul, as if he knew that he was an inconvenience, an oddball; as if he knew that I would quite like him to go away.

He couldn't be an angel, could he, showing up as he does every time I wax eloquent or seriously pray about evangelism? A grubby, unwashed angel, with gall bladder problems and a Methadone dependency? A seraphim with a yin/yang ring and a heavenly disinterest in fly buttons and toothbrushes? No, he's probably not an angel.

He is Jesus, according to Jesus. Giving him a cup of cold water, or the time of day, is like giving the same to Christ, according to the Gospel. Of course, in that sense, 'Grin' with the St Trinian's voice is Jesus too. Bias to the poor does not permit us to be prejudiced against the rich: all need the gospel.

Smashing pots and yelling in tongues is easier, but we talked back and forth, 'Train Man' and I, and Worthing came again, and he went again – no farewell wave this time. And as the train jolted and shuddered its way to London, I wondered what the world would be like if every Christian on earth treated every other human being as if they were Jesus himself.

Revival?

PLACARDS AND GUMMY PREACHERS

I keep bumping into confrontational evangelists. I recently took a tube journey, which included a chance encounter with a toothless herald of the gospel. As I lined up to get my ticket, a brother who was seriously challenged in the molar department came down the queue.

'Who's a believer here?' he hissed, quickly adding, 'There's heaven, and there's hell. Choose Jesus!'

He clutched a folder, which contained gaudy, medieval portrayals of both destinations. He opened the folder and flicked quickly through plastic-covered snapshots of sinners being barbecued forever and poked around with pitchforks.

'Where's it to be, then, heaven or hell?' he demanded.

A nervous lady said that she only wanted to go to Upminster. I fled.

It happened again in a local shopping centre. A small, grey man stood ramrod straight, with his right arm held aloft. His gloved hand defiantly clenched a huge placard. I sneaked a look at his poster. 'Repent Ye!' screamed the thick, gothic text. 'The end is nigh'. I cast my eyes downwards again, hoping to hurry past the brave little man, but it was not to be. His was a multi-media presentation: placard *and* voice. It was a big, fearful boom from one so slight.

'The Lord is not mocked' he thundered. 'Hell is a reality! Turn from sin today!'

My head down/rush past strategy failed dismally. He caught

19

my eye, and a laser beam of penetrating interrogation shot into my soul from his direction. '*You* sir . . . where will *you* spend eternity?'

I wasn't in the mood for a warm brotherly conversation at 300 decibels, and I didn't have a poster, so I mumbled 'heaven, thank you' and fled for cover into a shop.

In the bright warmth of the shop I felt safe again, but somewhat pursued by questions, and not questions about my eternal destination. As I peered out of the window at the grey man who was now barking at another terrified prospect, a blanket of unease shrouded me. He was undeniably brave, standing out in the cold with his dog-eared poster, but was he wise? Was this provocative style of his really bringing any *good news* to people, or did it just repel passers by like a swift apocalyptic kick in the teeth? Was this the way Jesus would have proclaimed his message, or did the man look more like one of the angrier Old Testament prophets? I believe that there is a hell to be shunned, and so it could be argued that mugging shoppers with the message is appropriate, but is hell the cornerstone of our message – or is that honour reserved for Jesus himself?

As I rambled absent-mindedly around the shop, looking for absolutely nothing at all, I searched deeper into my own concerns and questions about evangelism. With all of our 'seeker-friendly-be-culturally-relevant-bring-good-news-not-bad' approaches, we must face the fact that most of us Christians feel intimidated, uncomfortable and unsure about the best way to effectively share our faith with people.

I have had brief flirtations with just about every evangelistic 'approach' there is. I went through a phase when I really felt that I was doing God and God's world a massive favour, as I buttonholed people with my message, eager to capture as many 'salvation scalps' as possible. I tried the utterly unsubtle approach with my, then non-Christian, father. My warm attempts at sharing the love of God went something like this:

Dad: Quietly reading the newspaper, saying nothing. I enter the room.
Jeff: 'Hello, Dad. As you know from the contents of my daily
evangelistic monologue, I am a Christian, as per the copy of *Journey
into Life*, which I helpfully left under your pillow, just in case you
should come to your senses during the night hours. You, *sadly*, are not
currently listed among the elect. You are therefore destined for a long
swim in the lake of fire. Have a nice day.
Dad: Quietly continues to read the newspaper. I exit the room.

But then we can swing wildly to the other extreme, where we live
out the good news in our communities, happy that we are being
'salt and light', but never actually mentioning anything about
Jesus in the process. We congratulate ourselves on our 'cringe
free evangelism': any outsiders think that we're nice and even
rather cool, but never get to meet the Jesus who died and lives to
save them. We run the risk of becoming evangelical liberals: do-
gooders without a reason or explanation for our goodness.

My bookshelf is crammed with books telling me the right way
to do evangelism. But I just know that if I weren't a Christian, I
wouldn't want to be someone's project. I wouldn't want to be on
the receiving end of a monologue where I was barely given room
to respond. I wouldn't want to be told that my views were going
to be used in a survey which didn't actually exist – the 'survey'
being a made up ruse as an excuse for conversation. And I
wouldn't want to be patronised, press-ganged or threatened,
interrogated or intimidated, or made to feel that I knew nothing at
all about life.

Rebecca Manley-Pippert expressed something of the crisis that
many of us feel: 'There was a part of me that secretly felt
evangelism was something you shouldn't do to your dog, let
alone a friend.'[1]

So, would Jesus use the placard approach? He was not content
with impersonal messages; he didn't just send us a fax from
heaven announcing his love. Rather, he came among us; he came
down into our squalor and became a man. He refused to keep the

power of the Holy Spirit to himself, but dropped gentle prophetic exocets on the woman at the well during a lunch break.

Ask Jesus to help you be a good news message. Your friends (and maybe your dog) will thank you for it.

Note

[1] Rebecca Manley Pippert, *Out of the Saltshaker,* Inter Varsity Press, UK

WHO SWITCHED THE LIGHT OFF?

Airline seats are designed for people with only one buttock. I have a full set of two. I squeezed both of them into a seat on a flight bound for Manchester and searched quickly for the missing end of the seat belt, which had mysteriously disappeared beneath the person sitting next to me, who had apparently been blessed with five buttocks. I buckled up with a comforting click, and sighed with relief. I planned to make full use of the short one-hour flight. Time to read, nap, think, pray . . .

I took out my book (Christian), the aeroplane took off, and the flight attendants began their eager distribution of salted peanuts – ideal fodder for the dehydrated environment of an aeroplane. Suddenly, I became aware of the man next to me staring over my shoulder at my book page. I had become intimately acquainted with him, momentarily, in my seat belt search, but hadn't really noticed him. Lobbing another peanut into his mouth, he spoke.

'What are you reading?'

My brain leapt into gear, swiftly considering a suitable response. In a millisecond I contemplated the fact that my response should not be a cringy, in-your-face retort: *'It is in fact a Christian book, my friend, which leads me to ask, are you aware of your final resting place, should this fragile aircraft plunge to the earth and be consumed in a ball of white hot heat . . .?'* I had been preaching a lot about the need for Christians to be thoughtful and sensitive witnesses for Christ. In my early years as a believer, I was so keen to 'witness' that I would jerk any and

23

every conversation around to the subject of God:

'*Would you like a cheese sandwich, Jeff?*'

'*No thank you, for I have the Bread of Life . . .*'

So how could I answer this man's question concerning my reading material with subtlety? I cleared my throat, and responded:

'It's a book.'

The man gave me a look that he had probably not used since the sad day when he discovered he had been created with a bottom extension.

'Yes, I noticed that. What kind of book is it?'

Panic! How could I now proceed to disclose the subject of my reading without giving my fellow passenger the impression that he was parked next to an evangelical Hare Krishna?

'Eeeeer, it's a . . . quistion book' . . . (when you say the word 'Christian' very, very quickly it comes out through pursed lips as 'quistion'.

'Really. About what exactly?'.

'Um . . . about . . . Gd.' (the same principle applies to 'God' mouthed at speed).

'Right. So then, what do you for a living?'

Every muscle in my body immediately locked tight with tension.

'I, er . . . teach', I said, and inwardly congratulated myself on the answer, which sounded so much better than 'minister', 'vicar, sort of', or 'church leader'.

'Oh, you're a teacher then', he replied, instantly vaporising my sense of self-congratulation and causing fresh sweat to break out on my brow.

'No, I'm not. I . . . er . . . preach. Teach . . . about God.' And feeling a glimmer of boldness in my heart I added: 'I'm going to a Christian meeting tonight to speak'.

I settled back in my seat, and my interrogator went quiet – momentarily.

'And what exactly will you say to the people about God at

tonight's meeting?' he ventured. So I told him. He didn't cast aside his peanuts, hurl himself headlong onto the floor and cry out for forgiveness, but he did listen and ask questions, and I had the opportunity to spend some quality time passing on the great news of the love of God.

But, after I got off the flight, it occurred to me that the poor man had almost had to resort to torture and threat in order to get the gospel out of me. I was so determined to be laid back and inoffensive, that I had lost the eagerness to pass on the news that sometimes delights and sometimes offends.

Is it possible that we have lost sight of that issue called eternity, and the edge and urgency which that message conveys? In a reaction against 'pie in the sky' theology, with our emphasis on the kingdom being now, have we lost sight of the reality that we have a message that is bigger than life and death? Has the salt lost its savour?

Elton John did a nice job at the funeral of Diana, Princess of Wales. But with half the population of planet earth tuning in by television, we, the Christian church, who serve a Jesus, who calls himself the Light of the World, presented billions of people with a flickering, vague candle in the wind. But who am I to point the finger of criticism, if I am not willing, myself, to stick my beacon high on a hill, and pass on the good news with clarity, compassion and relevance?

Turn the light on, someone.

Note

Anecdotes used in this chapter have been taken from my book, *Gideon: Power from Weakness,* Kingsway Publications, 1999. Used by permission.

GIVE UP FLYING

The afternoon had begun quietly. Richard, my son, and I were cruising down Worthing High Street, on a regular sortie in search of CDs, stereos, and other paraphernalia that tends to fascinate the male of the species. Suddenly, I spied 'them'. Bandits at twelve o'clock, three hundred yards ahead: three Hare Krishnas. Oh, they were in disguise of course: no orange robes/drum under the left armpit/baldy heads for them. No, they were wearing flat caps and anoraks. But I immediately saw through their 'train spotters from Scunthorpe' attire. They were the Krishnas all right. Richard must be advised immediately. I hissed an urgent message out of the right side of my mouth.

'Look! Up ahead. Chaps with buckets who look like whippet fanciers. They're actually Hare Krishnas. Let's go in. Tally ho!'

Richard had been out shopping with me before, and so was a veteran of this kind of campaign. Weeks earlier, we had engaged another couple of low flying Krishnas in Chichester High Street, and had uncovered a somewhat dodgy ruse that they were using in order to solicit funds from unsuspecting civilians. Rattling their buckets under the noses of passing shoppers, they would request donations to help those with disabilities. It was a winning line; the buckets were brimming. Only Richard and I had discovered that the Krishnas didn't actually have a specific programme to help the disabled at all. They would use the money to give out Krishna indoctrination literature to the disabled, 'helping' them by inviting them to join up. So now, righteous

26

indignation fermenting in my bosom, I banked sharply and Richard and I went in for the first flypast.

The battle plan was simple. The two of us would maintain tight formation as we approached the enemy, and then would pull up sharply, without stalling of course, and slow down so as to give one of the collectors a chance to approach us. We would then have him clearly in our sights, and would be able to proceed to let him know that, despite his disguised fuselage, we knew his true identity, and then would let loose with the gospel cannon. Adrenaline pumped through my body as we went in for the kill.

We had to walk by three times before they took the bait. Finally, we approached them at a snail's pace, armed with somewhat foolish, cheesy, come-take-my-money-please grins.

It worked. Either the Krishnas hadn't noticed our triple bypasses – or perhaps they just thought that we were desperate to donate.

'Hello, sir, would you like to give some money to the disabled?'

Steady, now. Don't rush. Get him in your sights, control your breathing, and gently prepare to hit him with a scripture.

'Are you a Hare Krishna?' I enquired firmly, smug now – exhilarated even – knowing that this one was going to go down in flames.

'Yes, sir, I am,' came the expected reply – and suddenly, out of the blue, disaster struck; my brain froze; my mouth dried up in a second; my clever, cult-busting cannon jammed, and I couldn't think of a single coherent thing to say.

Richard looked at me, waiting for me to let the man have the first salvation salvo – but nothing came. All I could manage was a feeble, 'No, thank you.' It was time to get out of there, and fast. Signalling Richard to follow in my slipstream, I hurried away, hoping to melt into the crowd. It was not to be.

The Krishna was angry, so he shouted at my retreating back.

'Excuse me. EXCUSE ME . . . I am a PERSON sir, and you just treated me like a non-person sir, and I DON'T LIKE THAT.'

I stopped dead, and landed with a stomach-churning bump. Other shoppers halted too, and glared at me with loathing, as if I had bubonic plague and was on a mission to share it. I turned around to face the red-faced Krishna, his eyes wide with an offended stare. More slowly than the previous snail's pace, I inched my way back to him. Now was not the time to whip out a special anti-cult version of *Journey into Life*. Now was the time to apologise.

'I'm sorry. I'm a Christian, and I just behaved in a very stupid manner. I was ready to give you the Christian message with both barrels, but I couldn't think of what to say . . . I'm sorry that I treated you disrespectfully.'

Richard was stunned, and later reported the incident to his mum. 'Yeah, Dad spent ten minutes apologising to some bloke called Harold Krishna.'

And the man with the bucket taught me that, in our desire to be evangelistic, we should never treat people as projects, prospects, and certainly not as the enemy. People who are not Christians are not scalps, souls or statistics. They are human beings, with thoughts, feelings and opinions, invested with dignity by their Creator, marred by the fall, but people still.

I'm glad I met the Krishnas in Worthing.

I've given up flying.

THE FIRST TIME

My heart was beating wildly against my chest as I stepped into the crude, tin-roofed building. I stepped suddenly into a strange, alien world. A song leader with wild, windmill arms wrestled with a smile that threatened to possess his whole face. The congregation had eyes that were moist, and some of them had their arms raised up in the air.

Hands up? Who were they waving at? Were they asking permission to slip out to the toilet: one hand if you need go a little, two hands if you need to go, *right now*? Eyes shut tight now, some murmured quiet amens, others appeared to know how to speak Russian, or was it German? By now, I was succumbing to confusion, but it was to get worse. Abruptly the song ended, everyone sat down, and it was then that I saw it. Who in their right mind would build a miniature swimming pool in their church building?

The minister appeared, resplendent in a long black gown, with fishing waders up to his thighs – an aquatic dracula. Now another man joined him in the water. Suddenly, the Reverend Dracula grabbed the hapless guy and pushed him under the water. He had been baptised, and I'd had enough. I fidgeted though the sermon, made a mental note of how many people were desperate for the loo during the final song, and made a run for it. Sitting outside in my car, I decided: Christians were crazy. I would have nothing to do with them, ever again. Then I realised that I had left my coat in the church building.

I crept back inside, and was immediately assaulted by the youth leader. I had never seen so many teeth in a human head in my whole life. He invited me to the 'afterglow'. Now what? Did this crowd end their day by setting fire to old ladies? I walked in and joined the afterglowers. Dracula's victim approached me. Still wet, he shook my hand and got straight to the point. 'Hello. Are you are Christian?' I mumbled something pathetic, and suddenly realised that I didn't know God, and that I really wanted to. These people had confused me, irritated me, but I had to know the reason beyond their smiles. I told my still-dripping friend that I wanted to take the big step. His words chilled me:

'You have to go to the little room at the back'.

Horrors! Dracula would be there, in a room filled with stainless steel cabinets and glinting surgical knives. But in that 'little room' my damp friend explained the gospel without the aid of syringes or rubber gloves. Now it was 10 p.m., and I was a Christian. I stepped out into what I thought would be an empty church building. And then I saw them and heard the cheer. Every single member of that little congregation had waited to welcome me. With undisguised delight, they formed a long queue to the back of the building, and I slowly went down that line of love, hugged, and affirmed. I had found the church. They were a million miles from my culture, in just about everything they said and did. But they loved God, they loved one another, and they loved me. I was home.

REVIVAL IN WALFORD

Arthur Fowler is dead.

Arthur was not a 'new-church' leader, author, or Spring Harvest speaker. He was one of the major characters in the soap that I am addicted to – *EastEnders*. I am a pathetic individual. I actually cried when Arthur breathed his last – but then quickly recovered my composure when I saw his chest moving up and down two hours after his death. Maybe Reinhard Bonke had sneaked into the hospital . . .

But EastEnders has also just been blessed by the appearance of Walford Community Church. A group of intrepid church planters apparently sent from the planet Throg are meeting in Albert Square. Unfortunately they really do put the old cringometer in the red: a grinningly picture-perfect group in continuous ecstasy, they listen to the preacher with a rapt attention unknown in the history of Christianity.

Come to think of it, I used to believe that a church in revival would look like the Walford crowd. I had a utopian expectation of a revived British 'Christianville'. . . Steve Chalke – that incredibly anointed and appallingly handsome chap – chairing *Newsnight* perhaps? . . . The Prime Minister spotted speaking in tongues before rising for Question Time in the Commons, with MPs banging sticks during Madam Speaker's time of prayer? . . . Thousands of people rushing into our meetings begging for salvation, asking if they could stack chairs after all public meetings, and pleading to sign a covenant form. Of course, these myriads of chair stackers

31

won't need discipling . . . Trevor McDonald concluding *News at Ten* with 'Good night and God bless'. . . Thora Hird presenting *The Big Breakfast*?

But if revival isn't the above – then what is it? Before you reach for your spring-loaded Jonathan Edwards book, remember that most revivals don't exactly mirror previous revivals – God has this habit of being God. Then, there's no guarantee that we would automatically know if we were in revival. You can rent a royal, cut a ribbon, and declare a bridge open, but you can't declare a revival 'official'. Friends, following consultations with the Evangelical Alliance, the Spring Harvest executive, the Archbishop of Canterbury and the Apostles and Prophets Together for the Universe forum, I am pleased to announce that we really are in revival.' Posterity usually makes that particular judgement call. Often, we don't realise the significance of the current season that we're in. When David woke up on the morning of his epic punch-up with Goliath, he had no idea that the dawn was rising on 1 Samuel 19:

> David: 'Morning Dad. What chapter is it?'
> Jesse: 'Well, he who will shortly become a major hero, it's chapter 19.'
> David: 'Pops, what exactly is chapter 19?'
> Jesse: 'It's the part where you give a rather ugly giant a radical haircut, starting at the base of his neck, whereupon the people start chucking flowers at you and beg for your autograph.'

What really happened is that David wandered into yet another ordinary day, and God wandered into it with him.

Our struggle to define the word 'revival' is further compounded because the word is not specifically biblical – not that we should be too concerned – neither is 'Ford Escort', a very popular car among Christians. The word 'revive', on the few times it occurs, simply means 'life'.

But isn't the lack of a revival blueprint actually good news? Isn't it better that we walk into the future with the God of variety?

Revival won't be Utopia: it will mean incredible opportunity, but with pressure to match. A fresh gale of Holy Spirit-breathed life in the church, in the streets; a new sunrise of colour and creativity as the church rediscovers not only the black and white monochrome of words-only preaching, but the sights, tastes, smells and textures of the arts exploding in utilitarian 'new-churchism' once again.

Revival: it's an unknown quantity, but we live for it. We yearn for an explosion of life that will go deeper than the 'happy clappy' grins of Walford. And that's for real.

GROWING

HAS POTENTIAL

'Jesus looked at him and said, "You are Simon the son of Jonah. You will be called Cephas" ' (John 1:42).

Everything can change in a moment – particularly when Jesus is around. And just two words from his lips transformed the lives of a ragamuffin crew of ordinary people around two thousand years ago. He strolled up to some fishermen, their sweaty backs arched to the work of gathering swollen, waterlogged nets, and spoke the invitation: 'Follow me'.

A tax collector, crouched over his table, eyes shrouded with shame, nobody's friend really, heard the same whisper: 'Follow me'. And everything changed, because 'Life' began.

Just two words. In calling those first few, Jesus didn't set out a stall, spread forth a manifesto, present a plan or a strategy. Rather, he requested the pleasure of the company of Peter, James, John and Matthew, at a mobile kingdom banquet. And what a party it would be. The dead would wake up and dance to its music, the deaf would hear its rhythm, and the blind would see colour and contrast again. Those who had known only doors slammed in their faces by mere religion would join in the merry jig. Water to wine, bread for five thousand, ladies of the night now guests of honour at a table of righteousness and joy. And it all began with 'Follow me'.

Did the disciples ever daydream about what might have been if they had not 'happened'to bump into Jesus? He was their pivotal point, their junction, their revolution-packed-into-a-second. Thirty seconds after meeting Jesus, *everything* was different, normality

would never been seen again. Two words from him, and survival
gave way to living, darkness fled at the sudden dawn of light: a
cataclysmic change, so utterly total that he described it as being
reborn; the extinction of a life and the nemesis of a new order.

Potentiality was packed into the encounter. Jesus saw who and
what Peter was, but he wasted absolutely no time in letting the
burly fisherman know that there were plans afoot: plans to
transform him into somebody beyond his own wildest dreams.
Peter might have been just another anonymous nobody, a blue-
collar worker who lived out his days, quietly and uneventfully, a
life now buried beneath tons and tons of history's dust. He might
have become a spectacular sinner, an adulterer or a petty crook,
supplementing the leaner fishing days by connivance or deceit.
Potential for good or ill lives in every one of us, but when we
meet Jesus, we unlock the door to a higher kind of life – a living
that is a stratosphere above mere survival.

Stop and think about you, believer. Ever wondered about what
you might have been if you hadn't bumped into Jesus? I've been
wondering about me. Who might I have married, and would the
knot still be tied? I went into full-time Christian ministry at
twenty-two years of age. What would my career path have been,
and would I have found it satisfying? And what about my
capacity to consider the real meaning of life? If I had not become
a Christian, how would I have dealt with the hollowness of
Christ-less living? Would I have buried my questions beneath a
'go to work, to get the money, to give you the strength, to go to
work, to get the money' kind of existence. Would I have dulled
the ache with drugs, alcohol or loveless sex?

And I nearly missed Jesus. I came so close to walking away
from the big invitation. The day I became a Christian, I had
stormed out of a little church in East London, swearing and
cursing, vowing never to return, convinced that all of the
enthusiastic worshippers should be committed to a mental
institution, so off-put was I by their bright, glad madness. I
remember jumping into my car, lighting a cigarette, swearing

profusely once more, and declaring to a friend: 'That's beeping well it, I'm never beeping well going back into another beeping Christian church as long as I beeping well live . . . they're all beeping crazy. . . .'

And then I realised that, in my hurry to escape, I had left my coat back in the tin roofed building. There was nothing else for it – I would have to venture back into the zoo once more. I hurried back into the foyer, to quickly grab my coat so that I could get out of there and never go back.

But the grinning youth leader was waiting for me, a smile that displayed more teeth than Jaws and a ridiculous invitation on his lips.

'Hello again!' he cried with obvious glee at seeing the pagan Lucas return, 'Would you like to come to the afterglow?'

Afterglow? I was really confused now. No, I didn't want to go anywhere, thank you, except for the nearest pub, where a large Scotch would drown the thought of God forever. All I wanted was my fugitive coat, and as for the afterglow, were they setting fire to the old ladies or something? *'Throw Sister Doris on now, boys, she's a big girl, and she'll burn well . . .'*

My brain said pub and coat. My mouth said yes please, I'd love to go to the afterglow, thank you. And thirty minutes later, my bewildered friend and I knelt in the vestry wondering if the minister really did put his vest on in there, and asking Jesus to take charge of our lives. My friend had come in from the car as a one-man search party to extract me and had ended up staying too and he also became a Christian. In a minute, everything changed. I'd had my own 'follow me' encounter.

Twenty-six years later, I'm so glad that I didn't miss the moment. Calvinists will undoubtedly tell me that God would have found another way to get me to bump into him, but I'm not so sure. I'm glad that Jesus took charge back then. I'm glad he saw not only me as I was, but what I could become. I'm glad that I forgot my coat.

LISTEN

It had been a long flight to the USA. Flying in coach class makes you feel like you've had your legs wrapped around your neck for nine hours, and offers food that looks like an aerial view of a farmyard. I rented a car, and advised the car hire lady that, no, I didn't need any instructions on how to operate the car. I knew better. Right!

I drove south into the moonless night, blinking back sleep. It was well after midnight as I arrived in the darkened little Oregon city. I was to stay overnight with a couple, Chris and Jeanne, who have become our closest friends. Parking my car outside their house, I realised that town-wide snoring was in operation: I would need to be very quiet as I unloaded my bags.

Seconds later, as I opened the back door of the car, life got very loud. A deafening alarm system had been thoughtfully provided in my rental car, designed to alert extraterrestrials in other galaxies that the car was being stolen. All over the town, otherwise nice people were waking up swearing. I panicked, and began running laps around the vehicle – an excellent strategy for emergency situations!

Inside the house, my friends, hearing the cacophony outside, turned to each other with a knowing smile, and said, 'It appears that Jeff has arrived'. Chris came running out in his socks (he actually was wearing more than just socks, but you know what I mean).

'Hi Jeff, welcome to America. Quick, hop in the car', he screamed, above the nuclear early warning system that was now screaming from my car bonnet. Having wakened the neighbours in the immediate vicinity, we now proceeded to go on tour through the rest of town. Lights were coming on in previously darkened houses. The alarm was getting louder and was now screaming its way through an extended repertoire of deafening melodies. We pulled onto the darkened forecourt of a petrol station, minds racing. Let's disconnect the battery, I said. No, let's check the manual, he said. Let's run some more laps around the car, I said. No, let's call the car hire company, he said. And then Chris glanced at the car keys clutched in my sweaty palm, and his eyes narrowed.

'Jeff . . . is there a panic button on that key fob?'

I replied that, yes, there was indeed a button with the word PANIC printed neatly beneath it.

'And do you think, Jeff, that you might have pressed that button accidentally, oh you with the brains of a gerbil?'

I confirmed that this might possibly have been the case. I pressed the button again. Serene silence broke out as the alarm abruptly died, and a beautiful peace was once again ours. A police car, undoubtedly summoned to the disturbance, cruised by. We ducked behind the dashboard: noise criminals on the run. And suddenly, I remembered the kindly lady back at the car hire place who had tried so hard to give me instructions – but I had been too tired, too convinced of my own knowledge, too confident to listen.

Listen to God. Listen to your friends. Listen to your enemies sometimes, too. They may not like you, and their words might come wrapped in the unattractive packaging of unkind criticism, but they may bring you some life-changing truth.

Listen. It's better than running laps.

UNDER CONSTRUCTION

We've just, as they say, had the builders in. Actually, the builders were 'in' for eighteen months, so they really became permanent residents. It all began quite well: a jolly chap with the obligatory low slung Levis arrived. He possessed the sideways smile of a stereotypical 'builder's bottom' large enough to conceal a huge selection of Black & Decker power tools. He had a smiley face too, as he demolished our home and tut-tutted over the 'Mickey Mouse' efforts of various builders who had done previous work on the house.

I was immediately filled with admiration for the skills of our intrepid builder. DIY is not, as we Christians would say, 'part of my gifting'. This means that when I attempt to put shelves up, the entire family begins screaming intercessory prayers in high pitched, frantic unison. Electrics are a particular challenge. I can never remember the correct colour sequence to wire up a plug, which is why I nearly killed my mother when she put the kettle on. At least she got a free perm, but the smell of burning hair lingered for days.

Just about everything has worked out okay, except the new chimney that was constructed. It works fine as long as there is not enough wind to cause a feather to tremble, even slightly. The slightest breeze, however, which has been known to gust in our bracing winter climate, causes thick, acrid black smoke to bellow into our sitting room. Gas masks are not an option, and it's a bit boring watching television when you can't actually see the television set for the smog.

The smog wasn't the major cause of our stress, though. It wasn't the pitter-patter of hobnail boots on the stairs, the seventeen million cups of tea made, or the interesting turn of phrase employed by our faithful artisans when they had occasion to strike their thumbs with their hammers. The big stress was not generated by their optimistic 'always-look-on-the-bright-side-of-life' philosophy, which insisted that a three-inch gap under an ill-fitting door would, in fact, improve air circulation. It wasn't even the fact that we had more dust than the average sawmill on our stairs and in our lungs.

No, the stress came from being in a continual state of process. We lived in a perpetual condition of being 'almost there' and our sometimes lacklustre cry was, 'not-long-to-go'. In short, our house felt forever unfinished.

A similar frustration greets me just about every morning when I blink my eyes open and begin another day of being an incomplete person, a human being under construction. A journey can be an exciting thing, but every now and then, I wish that I was not 'on the road' to mastering some basic skills in prayer, but that I'd actually reached at least a 'Little Chef' of spirituality and could rest up for a while.

Perhaps it's as well to know that God is not waiting for me to be complete before loving me. He considers me his workmanship: scaffolding, broken tiles, wonky bricks and all. And he seems to understand my getting bored with the dirt, dust and debris of the never ending remodelling of my life – which is why Scripture encourages us to keep plodding on in the race set before us. 'Be patient, God isn't finished with me yet!' is not just another cheesy Christian slogan or a cop-out for stupid behaviour. The people around you, who have the capacity to make you scream, should probably be wearing a red triangular road sign round their necks – as should we all who are his apprentices.

'Take care – God at work.'

THE ROAD LESS TRAVELLED

I, ladies and gentlemen, am now a fully paid up member of my local gym. I have paid the joining fee, and now a weighty standing order hits my account every month, hard evidence indeed of my athletic ambitions.

My joining the 'Lycra Set' was long overdue. My belt was running out of expansion holes, and not only were my feet disappearing behind my expanding waistline, but children and small animals were found taking shelter beneath the shadow of my belly. I was getting breathless every time I opened my Bible. A page flip from a gospel to an epistle was okay, but turning from the Old Testament to the New really taxed me to the limit, and I knew that the use of a large concordance might actually take me out. My physical exercise was limited to building up the muscle of my right arm as a result of lifting hamburgers to my mouth. Something had to be done.

I donned my ancient sports gear, which was probably in fashion when Roger Bannister was at his peak, and headed for the torture chamber for my 'evaluation'. A grim-faced instructor with a permanent 'who's-been-a-naughty-boy-then' expression made me run on a treadmill, puff into what looked and tasted like a vacuum cleaner hose, and passed a few watts of electricity through my frame in order to measure my body fat. The result proved that just about everything except my toenails was, in fact, top quality lard. And so he prescribed a rigorous daily routine that would turn me into Bruce Willis, courtesy of stepping machines, rowing contraptions that bite your shorts when you push back, and a demonic bike which is always pointed uphill.

So now I have the key to a hard body. And you all know what's coming next, because I meet lardy gym members everywhere I go. I've been twice. The first time I loved it, and decided to turn my back on Christian ministry in order to pursue a distinguished athletic career. Why, I would visit the gym *twice* daily, not once. Soon I'd be a muscle-bound stud who could hand out Christian literature on the beach and kick sand in the face of any heathen who refused the tract held in my manly hand. The second time, I hated every second. I staggered out of the gym, face flushed blood red, chest heaving, frantic for oxygen, a picture of ill health.

And I've not been back. I think about going back every day, of course, and a guilty wave hits me. I overcome this by being in denial. I refuse to purchase larger clothes. My gym membership card sits in the back pocket of my jeans, which are *very* tight, because they carry a waist size something close to the measurement of my upper thigh. I aspire to fitness, believe in fitness, and long to be fit. I just don't want to take the steps needed to get me from aspiration to achievement.

The same sad, flabby situation often exists in my spiritual life. For some reason, I want to believe in effortless maturity, development and growth without cost, resolve or decision. I confuse salvation, which is mine without cost to me, through shed blood, with sanctification, which demands purposeful discipline. Holiness is a thousand choices.

Paul the apostle told his disciple and friend Timothy to 'train himself for godliness'. The word train in the Greek is *gumnaze*. Sound familiar? Yes, this is the root for our word 'gymnasium'. He's letting Timothy, as well as us, know that maturity isn't automatic. We will need to get down to the gym, as it were, and embrace grace-inspired discipline without legalism, if we want to sport some spiritual muscles.

Time to go. I have a pressing engagement with a demonic bike.

PICK ME PLEASE!

Our loft is a disaster area. Suitcases that will never see the light of day again battle for space with piles of fading photographs. There are a few horrendous wrought iron table lamps, the design work of tortured souls: lamps that should never, ever have seen the light of day in the first place. Our loft looks like the aftermath of Armageddon.

It was during my last excursion up in the rafters that I discovered my old school football boots. Running my fingers along the tired, cracked leather, still caked with mud from thirty years ago, I remembered one awful day in my inauspicious soccer career. The match itself had been a disaster for me: ten minutes into the game our sports teacher/referee had brought the entire match to a halt to ask me why I was playing in the position of centre forward when I was supposed to be a defender. I blush easily, and that day I glowed like a traffic light as I walked slowly back to my right back position. But the event that is really etched on my memory happened before the game itself – when the teams were being picked. Do you remember the routine from your soccer/netballing days? Two captains, impossibly intrepid athletes themselves, stand apart from a motley crew of potential team-mates, who are looking with pleading eyes; hearts crying 'Pick me – please'. Obviously, the best players are snapped up quickly, leaving a depressing group of apparent misfits who become more desperate to be selected by the second. Just four of us were left, then three, then two, then . . . me. One of the captains wrinkled his nose, like he was viewing the last turkey in the shop and said, 'oh well . . . we'll take Lucas then'. Blushing time again.

I'm not getting precious about this moment in my personal history. Excruciating as it was then, I don't think the experience has marred my psychiatric health. But as I sat in the half-light of the loft, and held the old boots again, I remembered for a moment the shame of being the player that no one wanted: reluctantly chosen because nobody else was available.

Then I recalled some words of Jesus that should cheer up any of us with less than brilliant sporting achievements: 'You did not choose me, but I chose you' (John 15:16). Ordinary, messed up people like loud-mouth Peter and wondering Thomas, and even traitor Judas were picked out of the crowd and given the invitation that changed a lifetime, an eternity, not just ninety minutes. They were chosen to be his disciples, his apprentices – and he's picked us for his team too.

It's remarkable that he's drafted us onto his team. After all, he's the coach who sees every weakness we have. We may fool the crowds, but he sees our clumsy, pathetic attempts in sharp focus. We miss our goals, and find it so easy to foul, and he watches it all. He knows us, and still likes us. And he has paid the highest transfer fee in history – his own life, his own blood shed – so that we could play on his side.

The problem is, knowing how to play on the Jesus team. What does it mean to be a disciple of Jesus? I've often thought that it was easier for the likes of the Twelve – because their selection was made by a physical Jesus, and they literally had to put aside their nets or tax collecting and be with him. For us, it may seem a little more complicated. Some suggest that discipleship means that we have to sell everything and give all we own away – but how can that really work? How can we follow Jesus in a world where ethics and goodness and values are scorned, and where spirituality is fashionable, but Christians always seem to get the red card?

Is discipleship a lofty term that can really only be used to describe the martyrs of yesteryear or the suffering church of today? We had better get this sorted out, because the Jesus who has picked us has commanded us to go and develop other apprentices for the team (Matthew 28:19). As we look at Jesus and discipleship in John's gospel, we'll discover that the life of discipleship is not a dreamy ideal for desert monks and missionary pioneers, but it's a way of life that is accessible and available to all of us.

If we're called to make disciples, that means that others should be involved in making us into disciples too. 'He Is All I Need' is a very old song that celebrates the idea that we don't need anyone in our lives except God himself. It has a nice, lilting tune, but the idea is theologically bankrupt. We do need other human beings to help us to become the disciples that Jesus wants. That's why church is more than a singing club or a biblical lecture centre – it's to be the discipling community, the forge where people of character and significance are crafted.

Personally, I think the discipleship ought to include volunteering to help clear up other people's lofts. Come on over. There's a free table lamp in it for you . . .

THE JOURNEYING GOD

I wish I had been there.

It was a hot Sunday evening, the pews were packed, and it was time for the closing benediction. The minister, splendidly sombre in black suit and stark white clerical collar, stepped up onto the platform, and stood majestically in front of the open baptismal tank. Minutes earlier, a number of grinning new Christians had breathlessly shared their testimonies and then had stepped down into the chilly waters. Now it was time to draw the evening to a close.

'The Lord bless you all', said the Pastor, smiling benevolently down at his flock. 'I'll see you next week . . .'

And with that, he stepped back, straight into the tank. I wish I had been there to see it. He was unhurt, and graciously joined in with the peals of delighted laughter as he beat a soggy retreat to the vestry. I love it when things 'go wrong' in church . . .

I wish I had been there when the rather overweight and over-bearing worship leader, whose 'worship leading' style was to bark orders at the congregation, demanded that they lift their hands, now! . . . And then, as he lifted his hands, his groaning belt buckle exploded and his trousers fell to his ankles, revealing a rather voluminous pair of boxer shorts apparently manufactured by Mr Walt Disney. I'm told that members of the congregation were sticking Bibles in their mouths in vain attempts to contain their mirth.

But my favourite 'things that go wrong in church' story took place in the USA, at a large nativity concert. Our American cousins are famous for their mega-productions: rented camels and donkeys, a full orchestra, and the ability to fly 'angels' across the church building, suspended by wires, sixty feet up in the air. The velvet-clad choir sang, eyes shining, the musicians played, note perfect, and the camels helpfully controlled their bowels. It was a beautiful moment, as at last the time came for 'Gabriel' (Norman the hapless deacon who had been volunteered) to appear. The crowds gasped as he rapidly swept high across the auditorium . . . and then glorious disaster stuck. The electric motor driving Norman's harness burnt out, and he stopped dead, so suddenly, that he began to swing wildly. And then, because of the momentum, the wires attached to angel Norman's wings got twisted, and he began to spin round and round, faster and faster. I wish I had been there to see that angelic ceiling fan.

But consider that vivid picture, of a man spinning round and round and round and round . . . and know that 'spinning' is exactly the condition that describes many Christians. The 'spinning' saints aren't overtly rebellious, out of fellowship, or prone to shake an angry fist at heaven. They are nice, good people, with heads filled with sound doctrines and hearts that are, as they say, in the right place. It's just that, spiritually, the 'spinners' aren't going anywhere. Progress has halted. Growth has faltered. Their Christianity has become stale and static. It can happen to the best, this 'spinning'.

Consider a ramshackle band of Hebrew slaves who, around 3,500 years ago, cried out for God to deliver them from the barbed whips, narrowed eyes and gritted teeth of their Egyptian taskmasters. God danced once again into their history as rescuer and redeemer, and the great journey – the Exodus – began. It was much more than a great escape. These outcasts and fugitives became a 'chosen' people, called to travel to a 'promised' land, and, initially, it was an action-packed journey. The 'Prince of Egypt', Moses, walked away from the good life of Pharaoh's palace in order to lead them. Their route wound its way through the supernatural and the miraculous, as the obedient Red Sea stood up, impossibly, at Moses' command, only to crash fatally down again on the vast army that chased them. God himself was their navigation system. As the Hebrews followed the pillars of fire and cloud, they discovered that Yahweh was, uniquely, the dynamic, travelling king. What a contrast to the pagan religions of the day, which held no long-term hope for the future and no plan of things. Paganism and the occult arts offered dark magic rituals designed to persuade the 'gods' to give you a good crop that year: manipulation for the sake of the immediate. But the Hebrews were called to follow the journeying God, the divine trekker, who rode daily at the head of his people. The Ark of the Covenant would be kept in a tent as a living reminder of the God who was committed to 'tenting it' with his people. Towards the end of the Judges' period, the ark was placed in a permanent structure, but the feeling remained that the proper housing for the throne of Yahweh was a tent.

But the story of those early travellers did not end happily. As they doubted, grumbled, and rebelled, they got more and more off course. God was still with them, but they would never inherit the Promised Land destiny that he had prepared for them. The journeying God allowed them to spin out their days in the wilderness, marching still, but going nowhere: a forty-year un-magical mystery tour. Even Moses was to die with the Promised Land just a distant horizon: the excursion ended in the sand.

So what of us, three and half millenniums later? Many of us have known an 'exodus' as we have stepped away from our Egypt: we have walked away from Godless, hopeless lives. Some of us have heard the call of the journeying Jesus who still says, 'come, follow me'. Others who have sat slumped by the roadside for too long, who have been spinning our wheels, will stir once more and take his hand: a firmer grip this time. Perhaps the Great Adventurer will come and invite us to get rid of excess baggage that weighs us down, or free our feet from the sin that so easily entangles, tripping us up just when we get moving.

What's it to be: onward, upward, to the promised land, or meandering around in the sand? Progress – or spinning? The journeying God warmly invites us to decide.

HONK IF YOU LOVE JESUS

It's a hot sticky summer's day, and I'm stuck somewhere on the M25. The traffic, as usual, is crawling. Bored, I look around at my fellow travellers, as drivers sit tensely tapping steering wheels, investigating their nostrils, or singing loudly along with Capital Radio. Something is different today. I suddenly notice that lots of the cars have fish badges on the back, and I'm reminded of the silly joke:

Question: How can you tell if a fish is a Christian?
Answer: Because it's got a car on its bottom.

I don't laugh, one doesn't while stationary on the M25.

Look! There's another 'Christian' car – apparent by the vast assortment of fading stickers on the back window:

'We're Going To Spring Harvest', 'We've Just Been To Spring Harvest', 'Only A Year To Go Before Another Spring Harvest', and very helpfully, 'In The Event Of The Rapture This Car Will Be Without A Driver'.

I'm relieved – the car has got a driver, so I've not been left behind, and I realise that I'm in a Christian traffic jam – or perhaps people are taking part in a prayer drive around the Capital: a 'Crawl for Jesus' event on the M25? A window is lowered, and a faint waft of Kendrick's new album, *Now That's What I Call Make Way* reaches me.

And then the penny drops. It's summer time, and that's when

52

thousands of Christians break in new sandals and shoot off to one of the many large Christian events that are held up and down the country. There are loads to choose from, catering for every taste. Loading up tents, caravans and, if you're a fully-fledged charismatic like me, a trailer for the worship flags. We trundle off and drive for miles in the hope of sunny days and encounters with God.

Pilgrims to Christian events are usually a patient crowd. It's not easy driving for ten hours, not being able to shout at other drivers because of that fish, and then arriving at your chalet/shed which, as they say, is missing one of two minor items – like a sink and a front door.

And then there's the weather. A couple of years ago, an incredible freak windstorm hit a large Christian event. One or two happy campers who were walking to the large tent suddenly found themselves sitting in a tree, no doubt wondering if the Lord had miraculously transported them there. And then of course, there are the toilets, for which Greenbelt used to be particularly famous. If a person fell down in that pit, mercy would demand that they just be shot.

Of course, all of these events need teachers and preachers to provide the instruction and inspiration, which can be hard work, particularly when an event runs a number of repeat weeks. I spent four weeks speaking at Spring Harvest one year. For months I would wake up in the middle of the night screaming 'Shine Jesus Shine' at the top of my voice . . .

So what's the point to it all? Critics of the event sub-culture tell us that it would be better to stay at home and reach out to our communities rather than waste time on 'Christian' holidays – and they probably should add 'bah, humbug' to their scrooge-like criticisms. The fact is that it is a great idea to get away, sing some new songs, get inspired, and cremate some barbecued chicken with some friends. And God seems to work overtime as people take time out to meet with him.

In my early days as a Christian, I attended a church youth camp on the Isle of Wight. It changed my life. Yes, of course I was

somewhat zealous in my responses to the nightly preaching. I'd
go forward at the end of very sermon: if the appeal was given for
Cantonese dyslexic basket-weavers, I'd still go to the front, eager
for anything and everything that God had for me. But that
summer event played a formative part in my Christian
experience. That's why I'm convinced that these events are so
useful – because God goes along to them too.

Back on the M25, I've just responded to another Christian
sticker, inviting me to honk my horn if I love Jesus. I have
obediently honked, but judging by the swift gesticulation from
the driver, I must assume that he's not a Christian. Surely not . . .

SURVIVING CYNICISM

The preacher was really working up a sweat now. Fire dancing in his eyes, he hurried urgently along the long line of waiting, praying people, their hands extended before them, their eyes tightly shut, focused on another world. Within minutes, the worshippers became skittles; their bodies scattered haphazardly. Watching from three rows back, my mind raced. The scene was familiar enough to me. Over the last few heady years of renewal, I've been in hundreds of meetings where the Holy Spirit has swept through, bringing an overwhelming presence that literally sweeps us off our feet; and I've done a fair share of 'carpet time' myself. The crowded rug didn't trouble me. So, what was the source of this persistent, nagging, question mark that gnawed away at my brain, flitting around my head like a humming mosquito? My nervousness had begun earlier, during the preaching. Apparently, the speaker had just returned from 'phenomenal', 'extraordinary' meetings in India, where, and I quote, 'hundreds of thousands of blind eyes had been opened, and hundreds of thousands of deaf ears had been unstopped.' I had quickly stifled the irreverent thought that such an avalanche of miracles would surely have put the relatively unknown speaker on the front cover of *Time Magazine*.

Now, as he ministered, the nervousness returned. Why does he have to hit them so hard when he prays for them? That was it. I didn't mind his impassioned, theatrical shouts, 'In the name of Jeee-sus!' as he raced along, or the comical positioning of the catchers, as they tried to figure out which way each body was going to fall; their arms out, waiting for the next crumpling. I honed in on the source of the niggle. He was hitting them: ramming the palm of his hand into their forehead, and then pushing their heads back at an angle. My mind skipped and danced between anger and guilt. I was angry, and mildly depressed, at the apparent circus trickery, which so desperately needs someone to fall down that a good shove is in order, and full of guilt, for even thinking such a thing about this man of God – was this just his style? Closing my eyes, and covering my ears, I tried to pray, and hoped that it would be over soon.

I describe this real moment for you, because it demonstrates a common dilemma. How should we posture ourselves in these days of manifestations, miracles, stories of God at work from near and far, and hopes of revival? When God moves, some people clench their fists and fight what they don't understand, while others throw open their arms and seem willing to take on board anything that comes along. The country is littered with the cynical – and the naive.

We rightly fear cynicism: the cancer that so readily strikes the hopeful. The cynical heart is freezer-cold, unable to be warmed by the God who really does come and work among his people. Cynicism takes the tenderhearted worshipper and turns him into an arms-folded spectator, a scowling analyst with a stopwatch and clipboard under his arm, and a bless-me-if-you-dare expression on his face. If you question the power of cynicism, consider the Pharisees, who could watch – and smell – a foetid Lazarus, as he staggered out of his stinking tomb, and then rush off to plot the death of the Jesus who presided over that resurrection. They saw with their eyes, but cynicism blinded their hearts even to that starkest of miracles. Cynicism doesn't melt when the flames of revival ignite: on the contrary, it hardens in the heat. When God comes, the Pharisees get more pharisaic, and the hopeful become more hopeful – just check the gospel accounts. The cynic may smile a smug grin and feel that he is more mature than the rest of us naive simpletons, but he is in the grip of a disease and a delusion. There is only one cure for cynicism – we must repent of it. It is unbelief by another name.

But a simplistic, thoughtless naiveté is waiting for us at the other extreme. Unquestioning, we just take on board every prophetic word, regardless of content or spirit. A new 'revelation' is shared and, despite feeling an urgent sense of disquiet, we bury our concerns, not wanting to be perceived as critical or 'out of the flow'. This silent pressure to conform can be very intense in an atmosphere of spiritual enthusiasm, like a church pursuing revival. It's like being carried along by a huge football crowd: your shoulders are pinned tight; your feet lifted off the ground – a hapless passenger of the consensus. We feel guilty for even considering the possibility that something might be wrong. Surely, if everyone is going with it, they can't all be mistaken?

It's a most extreme example, but the fact is that everybody was wrong the day they drank orange squash laced with cyanide at the infamous Jonestown. But a similar power of peer group pressure can bid us to silence our questions and concerns. We don't want to line up with the critical people who rush to the publishers any time that God shows up – and we certainly don't like the Judas the traitor/Thomas the doubter feeling that rises up when we ask awkward questions. So we stay silent, and worry quietly.

Is there a pathway between these two extremes – a so-called 'healthy' scepticism? I believe that there is – and that there is a biblical demand that we walk on that middle ground. As Paul wrote to his friends at Thessalonica, we are to 'Test everything. Hold onto the good' (1 Thess 5:21). This command comes immediately on the heels of Paul's warning that we should not 'put out the Spirit's fire', or 'treat prophecies with contempt'. So, this testing is not seen as a negative, doubting response to the work of God, but rather, as a positive duty for those who would feel the heat of Holy Spirit flames and hear his voice through the prophets.

We create an environment where this testing can take place when we encourage people to ask questions, even difficult questions at times, in order to find clarity and authenticity.

Whenever God moves, question marks are scattered all over the place. The day of Pentecost brought an outbreak of power and a rash of questions and misunderstandings. 'What does this mean?' the crowd asked. We'd do well to take the time to join them. Sometimes, I wonder whether we Charismatics know how to *feel*, but not how to *think*. But Jesus told his wonderful little stories in order to provoke his listeners to questions, so that in the mental wrestling and the cut and thrust of debate, we discover.

Questions save us from gnostic meaninglessness. There have been quite a few times when I have wanted to interrupt a prophet who seemed to be making nebulous pronouncements: 'You say that we are on the edge of the third breakthrough in the heavenlies as we embrace the hallmark of the new thing God is doing for the hungry and thirsty. But what do you mean?' I am genuinely grateful to be part of the Pioneer network of churches, to be around passionate people who are fully committed when it comes to looking for God, and yet, unafraid of the awkward questions that help us as we search for him.

We will also need to guard our attitude as we question. Paul Reid says that churches are hindered by people who have 'an opinion about everything and a heart for nothing'. What is the motive, and the starting point for our questions. Do we enquire out of a desire to prove the badness of something – or rather its goodness? Perhaps that's my problem with some of those who have written so vociferously against Toronto, Pensacola, and anything else connected with revival. It seems that they begin with the premise that the thing is wrong, and then gather information to prove their point – their side of the story – rather than presenting a balanced analysis. Such an approach is unfair and inappropriate.

Cynicism also flourishes when our expectations are unrealistic: a common problem among idealists like us. We all have unspoken expectations about the way things should be, and rightly so. But we can forget that those that we walk with are flawed human beings – just like us. If you've been in a church for more than six months, and nothing about it and nobody in it has ever irritated you, then you're probably clinically dead. We do need to adjust our hopes into line with a realistic understanding of the frailty of human nature.

There's only one way to stay balanced on the tightrope between unbelief and unhelpful simplicity. It takes grace. And my conclusion on that heavy-handed evangelist? Well, he is anointed; I'd like to see some Indian medical reports; and he should stop shoving people around.

Note

Anecdotes used in this chapter have been taken from my book, *Gideon: Power from Weakness,* Kingsway Publications, 1999. Used by permission.

LESSONS FROM A CAR WASH

Be honest with me – do you ever just feel *ordinary*? It's not that
you have a major inferiority complex, it's just that you are very
aware that you not only have feet of clay, but that that most of
your body is made of that off-brown modelling material.

I had a crisis of feeling ordinary when attending a major
leaders' conference a few years ago. Even the names of some of
these conferences can be vaguely intimidating. This was called,
Bionic Apostles and Prophets Together for the Universe – or
something like it. I made my way to the dining room and sat
opposite a woman who looked incredibly mighty in God to the
pulling down of strongholds. She had 'WOMAN OF GOD!'
written all over her – a veritable Reinhardia Bonnke. She was
quietly eating the meal, which had been lovingly prepared for her
by the Christian Conference Centre *Chef de Cuisine*.

I immediately felt ordinary. This woman probably knew
Leviticus off by heart and cast out demons before breakfast. I
ventured to introduce myself.

'Er, hello, my name is Jeff . . . Jeff Lucas.'

I expected her to look up from her meal, heaven ablaze in her
eyes, and say with the authority of the sage: 'Yes . . . I know. I saw
you in a vision in 1953.'

She did not say anything of the sort. She just greeted me with a
bright hello and introduced herself.

'Have you had a good week?' I enquired. More for something
to say really.

'No, it's been terrible . . . awful in fact.'

I struggled to look compassionate and sympathetic, but inwardly my heart soared. Good! Ms Mighty in God had had a rough week. That meant that she was normal, and that all circumstances did not immediately jump to her intercessory command.

'Er . . . what went wrong then?' I asked hopefully.

The dear lady then described how she had taken her family to the car wash (which I thought was a bit sad: 'come on kids, let's break the bank and have some fun. Off to the car wash we go then.') During her attempt at these mechanical ablutions, family-style, a major personal crisis developed. It appears that Ms Mighty in God had put the token in, noted that gratifying moment when the big brushes obediently start spinning and the water jets begin to advance relentlessly towards you, and then decided to check that her car window was shut tight. She flicked the handle, which came off in her hand, and then, to her total horror, the window fell down all the way, disappearing inside the door, leaving a huge gaping hole which would surely facilitate the admission of thousands of gallons of warm, sudsy water. They would all be drowned! The woman looked around her car in a vain search for something, anything, to put into the gaping hole to prevent her car from becoming a cross between Noah's Ark and the Titanic. There was only one thing that she could find that would provide a suitable watertight seal . . . her own bottom.

I really tried not to laugh, but the very thought of it made me want to lie on the floor and kick my legs in the air. And part of my joy was the release that came in knowing that, yes, this was a woman who really loved God and had his authority upon her life. And this was a person, who, just like me, knew how to do idiotic things, knew how to be absurd, probably knew how to be scared, and knew how to be defeated. She was ordinary. I am ordinary. And so are you. But the extraordinary God that we serve seems to enjoy taking clay pots like us (the treasure of God being in 'earthen vessels') and using us as instruments for revival. That includes a 'mighty warrior' who was cowering fearfully in a winepress (Gideon), a stammering prophet who described himself as a bumbling pre-adolescent (Jeremiah) and a host of other no-hopers (in human terms) who ended up as highly effective instruments in the hands of our remarkable God. Feeling ordinary? Join the crowd.

Note

Anecdotes used in this chapter have been taken from my book, *Gideon: Power from Weakness,* Kingsway Publications, 1999. Used by permission.

EXCUSE ME, YOUR BOTTOM'S ON FIRE

The BMW was big, startlingly blue, and nothing short of beautiful. I admired it longingly, trying to erase words like 'covetousness' from my mind as I did. It belonged to Chris and Jeanne, two close friends.

Now I'm not normally a car fan. I scoff at television commercials that feature voluptuous ladies and slogans like 'Britain's Sexiest Car'. Perhaps there's something wrong with my hormones, but I confess that I never felt amorously stirred by a couple of tons of metal.

But this BMW was a beautiful thing. No hint of shimmer or wave could be found in the paintwork, just a flat, gleaming ocean of liquid glass in a rich blue sheen.

I eased myself onto the back seat, enjoying the luxurious smell of leather seats. The car purred as we began our journey; bumps and potholes in the road ironed out instantly by superb suspension. And then suddenly everything went wrong. Chris, the driver, noticed that the normally attentive controls were malfunctioning badly. The trip computer on the dashboard was manifesting in German, and made me remember my *Beano*-reading days (Achtung! Achtung! etc) I could smell oil, and felt the need to testify to this fact.

'I can smell oil' I remarked as casually as I could. Jeanne turned and looked back at me, and made a startling assertion. 'That's not oil, Jeff – your backside is on fire'.

It turns out that, earlier that day, a new battery had been fitted in the car, which, unusually, was sited under the back passenger seat – my seat. Unfortunately, the battery company had installed the wrong model, and so the terminals were sticking up a full inch higher than they should. So when I had planted my evangelical behind on the leather, the seat went down and the metal frame of the seat connected with the proud terminals, which shorted out. Now the battery was on fire, and the car's electrical systems were going swiftly into terminal meltdown. We quickly pulled the car over, jumped out at lightning speed, called the fire brigade and watched the beautiful machine go up in flames. Seconds later, it was a write-off.

Chris was insured, and said (very graciously) that he had never really liked the car anyway. I was stunned by my own lack in the self-awareness department. I had been surrounded by smoke – a miniature inferno was gathering heat beneath my rear end – and I hadn't noticed. It was left to my observant friend Jeanne to point out what should have been profoundly obvious.

Take a snapshot of the scene, and consider a parable. How often are we guilty of being blissfully unaware of the presence in our lives of all kinds of shortcomings, character flaws and sometimes downright sins? People around us marvel at our myopia, and are stunned that we seem blind to what is so very apparent to everyone else. Hopefully, we will have the grace to respond with gratitude and kindness, when, figuratively speaking, a friend quietly whispers: 'Excuse me, but did you know your backside is on fire?' How many once 'beautiful' lives now look like something of a write-off, simply because of a refusal to listen?

READING THE SCRIPT

It was a chilly Irish morning. My eyes flickered open, and I focused on the chalet ceiling. Where was I, and what was I doing here in this holiday shed? Ah, that was it. I was speaking at a conference in the south of Ireland – 'Together for the Kingdom'. A couple of thousand believers from both sides of the border had taken over a holiday camp for a week of teaching and celebration. The camp itself had seen better days – probably – but the sense of the presence of God around the place more than made up for the fading glory of the site.

Kay was still asleep, and Kelly and Richard were, apparently, also still in the land of nod. Time for a shower. The bathroom was at the rear of the chalet. This meant that I would have to circumnavigate my way out of our bedroom, across the sitting room/kitchenette, down the hallway and turn first left into said bathroom. Easy!

I didn't have any clothes on, but felt that it would be safe to sprint to the bathroom, after all, everyone else in the Lucas clan was fast asleep, so my naked expedition would surely go unnoticed. I inched quietly out of bed, opened the bedroom door, and began my goose-bumped trip. I had tiptoed half way across the sitting room when suddenly I heard the noise behind me. I froze. It was the sound of a door being opened – the front door of the chalet. I immediately had a double revelation. Firstly, I realised that I had failed to lock the front door before retiring for the night, and secondly, from the clatter of carts outside I realised that the cleaning ladies were doing their rounds. I was now in a major moral dilemma: in two seconds, I was going to have a naked encounter with a lady armed with a broom. Should I hurl my body up against the door, preventing the aforementioned lady from accessing our chalet and my nudity, or should I do a triple back flip into the well equipped kitchenette and find some utensil with which to retrieve my modesty? I needn't have considered either option, for there was no time: this was a turbo-charged cleaning lady. As I turned to face the opening door (mistake) she popped her head round, smiled sweetly, and looked me in the eye – for which I was most grateful.

I froze to the spot, and was speechless. We stood there, she and I, for what seemed about ten years, but it was only five seconds. I wondered what she would say. Would she apologise, scream, or laugh before beating a hasty retreat. A veteran cleaning lady like her had probably been in this position before, surely? But what would she say?

She acted as if there was nothing untoward at all . . . and then she spoke. Her words surprised me, to say the least.

'Good morning sir. Would you like me to change your sheets?'

I was stunned. Either this dear lady was a consummate professional, or she was just saying what she said about a dozen times every working morning of her life: 'Would you like me to change your sheets, would you like me to change your sheets, would you like . . .'

She was reading the script. Saying what she always said, doing what she always did. I found my tongue, thanked her for her offer, and advised her that I felt that our sheets were alright and could probably wait until tomorrow to be changed, thank you very much.

'Okay then, thank you', she smiled, and went on to the chalet next door. I heard her knock at the door, open it, and then call the same well-worn phrase 'would you like me to change . . . .' On with the script.

Another classic bit of script reading was observed during an aeroplane flight into Chicago. It had been a very long flight from England and I had been sitting next to someone with a child who should have been named 'Damien – child of the beast'. Sitting on my left was a good friend who had joined me for the trip. We were about twenty minutes away from landing at O'Hare International Airport when the pilot decided to make a special announcement.

'Pilot here. We have a slight problem. We are losing hydraulic fluid from the aeroplane. Actually, those of you seated on the right hand side of the plane may be interested to see it shooting out of the wing.' (I was sitting on the right side. I looked for the shooting liquid. It was indeed shooting.) The pilot continued: 'This little problem means three things. First of all, we can't get the flaps to work.' Great, I thought. This incey-wincey little problem means that we can't actually get the aeroplane to go downwards.

'Secondly, we can't get the landing gear to lock.' (Super. If we do manage to get the aeroplane to head down towards the runway, then we can't land the thing anyway.)

'Thirdly, we can't get the brakes to work'. (Hooray. If we do get down, and we do actually manage to land, then we can't stop. Praise the Lord!)

I felt inclined to pray at this moment, but have to admit that my prayer was somewhat high-pitched: a sort of Vienna Boy's Choir act of intercession. My friend wasn't as brave or as spiritual as I, and was attempting to climb into the overhead baggage compartment while screaming for his mother.

The pilot decided to reassure us. His first attempt at reassurance wasn't terribly successful:

'Don't worry everyone, they've closed the rest of the airport down and we do have fire trucks and paramedics standing by.' (How comforting. More muffled screaming for parental help from above.)

The pilot's second attempt at calming the jagged nerves of his passengers was received with greater enthusiasm:

'Don't worry, everyone. We've managed to operate the flaps, and we can come back there and pump the landing gear down by opening a little hatch in the walkway. We won't have any brakes, but we can throw the plane into reverse thrust and land quite safely. Please relax, we'll be fine'.

A wave of subdued relief seemed to sweep around the cabin, and cries of 'thank you God, I love you mum', were heard from the overhead baggage compartment, but a tension remained. As the descending plane approached the runway, we could see the red flashing lights of the emergency services – they weren't taking any chances. We went screaming down the runway, hotly pursued by eager fire trucks, and finally, after what seemed forever, we settled down to a halt right at the very end of the available tarmac. The plane was so in need of repair that a tow truck would be dispatched to tow us into the gate.

Relief swept the plane. The men who, five minutes earlier, were acting like gibbering chimpanzees, were now pretending that the whole thing had been a thoroughly wonderful adventure. They gave each other high fives and laughed just a little too loudly. The ladies were a bit more honest. They hugged each other, dabbed at tears and exchanged Body Shop products. It was a warming sight. And as my friend said his farewells to the overhead baggage and climbed back down to join me, I noticed the three nuns singing 'Kum By Ya' at the back of the plane.

Suddenly, the PA system crackled again. It was our intrepid pilot, with a few more words. As he coughed and cleared his throat, I wondered what carefully selected words he might use at this poignant moment. There we were, sweaty, traumatised, grateful to be alive: an episode that, surely, none of us would ever forget. What would the pilot say to sum up our feelings at that moment. Would he give thanks to God, or quote the poet Milton, the statesman Churchill, or some obscure Greek philosopher? He did none of these things.

'Hello, ladies and gentlemen, your pilot here. On behalf of the airline, I'd like to be the first to welcome you to Chicago. Do have a nice day. Goodbye!'

That was it! No thanksgiving, no apology, no epic speech for the moment of our deliverance. Just the normal bit of script reading that he always used every time he landed a plane. A few moments of pressure, and then he snapped right back into the well-worn routine.

We can all be quite proficient at script reading. Come to think of it, script reading is a part of life. We go to work to get the money to buy the food, to give us the strength to go to work to get the money, to buy the food . . .

Television advertisers provide us with compelling instruction on the art of living: we must surely have their product if we are to survive. Culture presses in hungrily, demanding that we wear that certain fashionable item of clothing, because those that produce that item insist that we do so. Unthinkingly, we march through life, reading a script that someone else has written, marching to a beat that is bashed out by an unknown drummer.

We live in an age of information overload – and a famine of reflection. And we Christians aren't by any means exempt from this mindless script reading. Some Christians would rather die than think. As Gerald Coates put it, 'some believers are so narrow minded, their ears touch.'

May God help us to engage the brain that he gifted us with, and break out of the numbing, slavish obedience to our culture's tinny jingles. God, help us to think.

REALITY

HAPPINESS IS REQUIRED

It all began with an innocent question. I asked the little man how he was. It was a mistake!

Moments earlier he had been perusing the contents of one of my books which were nattily displayed on a table at the back of the church building. His dark, eagle eyes darted over the flicked pages, in rapid search for potential heresy. He sniffed, dropped the book back on the table like a red-hot coal and barked back his retort.

'Me? Listen here, brother. I'm praising God. What about you?' There was no warmth in the voice, no gentle enquiry, but rather a screeching demand that made me want to scream, *'no one expects the Spanish inquisition . . .'*

Fearing that a less that gleeful response would prompt him to immediately remove my fingernails and immerse me in a huge vat of molten lead, I affirmed that, er, yes, I was indeed praising the Lord and beat a hasty retreat to the toilet.

Inside, a friendly looking man was washing his hands, which is a splendid idea in evangelicalism, where fraternal handshaking is a major pastime. Relieved that I had escaped from the book table and the official representative from the Waffen SS School of Hospitality, I blurted out, 'Hello . . . how are you?' Another mistake!

He smiled, and tugged at the demonised automatic towel, which automatically jammed. 'Oh, I'm fine, brother'. And then he added, a wistful look in his eyes, 'We *have* to be, don't we!' disentangled himself from Beelzebub the towelling machine, and left.

My mind spun wildly. First I had to meet Conan the barbarian worshipper, and then the kindly man with soggy hands made it quite clear that it is required of Christian types to be fine, happy, thrilled, ecstatic, *by order*. I returned to the hall, where the meeting was now starting, and a farmer was giving his testimony.

'Yes, this last week, I was kicked in the head by a sheep. *Praise God!*' he enthused, as if getting mugged by a skinhead fleece had long been the ultimate ambition in his life.

'Amen!' cried the congregation, suggesting that they too would love to be on the receiving end of a lamb chop – to the head.

'I 'ad to 'ave seven stitches in my left eye. Hallelujah!' he continued, to the further delight of the crowd, who were all apparently desirous to become in need of the assistance of Guide Dogs for the Blind.

I thought that this sort of 'my-legs-just-dropped-off-but-I'm-ecstatic' kind of Christianity had died out years ago. Back in the Seventies, when bright young Christian things like me were head-banging to Len Magee's 'He's Only a Prayer Away', we used to sing songs that celebrated the fact that we were all consistently, unstintingly thrilled.

> It isn't any trouble just to s-m-i-l-e
> No it isn't any trouble just to s-m-i-l-e
> If you pack up all your troubles
> Then they'll vanish like a bubble
> If you only take the trouble
> Just to s-m-i-l-e

But life, even the Christian life, is not a gallop from one thrill to another. There are the boring bits. Jesus *has* washed my sins away, but I still have to wash the car. Grinning with gritted teeth doesn't work when tragedy knocks at your door. Jesus didn't flash a cheesy smile and head-butt a tambourine in Gethsemane. He struggled, wept, ached, and argued – and stayed faithful to his father's will. He was open about his pain, begging his sleepy friends to watch in prayer with him.

Reality – not unending ecstasy – is required. And mint sauce as well. After all, there are some seriously dodgy sheep out there.

FAME

The two women are very, very large, and their anger matches their girth. Hatred blazes wildly from their eyes, obscenities and profanities come screaming from their lips: lurid, jagged missiles of spite. They have to be restrained now by bigger, burlier minders, as they kick and scream, and scratch and bite. They are on a mission to destroy each other, in the public weekly bloodletting that is the Jerry Springer Show. At the end of the show, Springer, the grand ringmaster of this voyeuristic circus, will spend a minute or two delivering a little homily that exhorts people to be good to each other. His saccharine message at the end of another round of relational destruction is a sickeningly pious moment. It's like putting 'Thought for the Day' at the end of the gladiatorial games. There's blood on the floor, relationships smashed forever to smithereens, and marriages doomed. And the hapless guests did it all for all for a brief moment of fame.

Perhaps Andy Warhol was right – we all want fifteen minutes of fame. The ill-fated Diana lived and died for it, hounded by the pack that she also loved to court. *Hello* magazine gives us blow by blow details of celebrity lives, and is more than able to pay a movie star a million or two for their wedding snaps. Such is our illogical hunger for a glimpse of the famous.

And now, we live in the era of the docu-soap: the prime-time transmission of the tedious. We are desperate to know just what an airport check-in person does. We are captivated by the daily schedule of a window cleaner. Ours is a culture that needs to get out more!

Fame is something that Christian leaders can be quickly drawn by, perhaps with a greater pull. Surely, the icons of our culture know that our interest in their clothing, their affairs, and their taste in food is a superficial thing: entertainment to distract us in our boredom. But the Christian leader is applauded for his or her spirituality: they are considered worthy icons to speak on matters of life and faith; they have the power to truly affect our lives. Fame crouches, waiting to bite at our heels as we preach another sermon on servanthood. We even have spiritual words for fame: 'profile', 'influence', 'broad effectiveness'. The Christian world is relatively small, and the well known are but larger goldfish in a tiny bowl. But fame can still be a temptation. Perhaps that's why Jesus teaches us to do our giving and most of our praying in private. The Pharisees would quite literally blow trumpets to announce that they were going to drop a few coins in the offering. The desire to be known, and particularly to be known for our piety, is no new temptation.

I've had a couple of conversations with God about fame. Both were at Spring Harvest, an event that gathers some 70,000 believers together annually. For a number of years, it had been my privilege to be involved in the youth programme of the event. It was my conviction then, and still is now, that the best communicators at Spring Harvest are to be found in the youth programme. It's one thing to stand up and wax eloquent to 5,000 people in an adult setting. They are braving the bracing winds of Skegness or Minehead because they want to hear what you've got to say. It's quite another matter to hold the attention of 1,000 teenagers, many of whom resent the fact that their fanatical parents have dragged them off to this Christian jamboree anyway. I am so grateful for the time that I spent working as a youth communicator, and I did not view becoming involved in communicating with the adults as some kind of step up the evangelical ladder. But I was struggling with a couple of issues. For one, I was getting older, and there was a desperate need for 'more seasoned' preachers like me to stand aside to let newer youth communicators come through. But I also had a sense that God had given me some things to say that might need a wider audience. I remember feeling frustrated, tagged as someone who could only have any relevance to youth. I went for an angry stroll on the 'glorious' beach of Skegness, and had a good moan at God about my feelings. No bright light dawned over the murky waves, and no angel strolled beside me as I shuffled through the shiny, wet pebbles. But it was as if a voice inside me – one that I've learned to recognise – asked me a very searching question as I picked my way through the flyblown piles of dried up seaweed.

'Do you want to step onto a platform that I have not prepared and lit for you?'

I knew it was God, challenging *me* about *me* pushing me, bidding me to wait for *his* timing rather than grasp for opportunity. I answered that, no, I didn't want to do that at all. Peace came.

A number of years later, God decided to throw the light switch into that area of ministry, and I began to contribute into the wider arena of Spring Harvest. I spoke one evening in the big top. It went well. Actually, it went very well. The content seemed to hit the mark, the presentation flowed, and the crowd obligingly laughed at all the funny stories. It was, as they say, 'a result'.

The next day, I strolled towards the team lounge for my morning dose of caffeine, and began to notice that I was being noticed. People nudged each other as I walked by, some smiled and said good morning, and others whispered, 'It's him – you know – last night'. I downed my coffee and wandered over to the bookshop; I had a few minutes to spare and planned a quiet, leisurely browse. But as I walked into the book area, I had to pass the booth where cassette recordings of all of the meetings were sold. A large sign was hanging up which said, 'Jeff Lucas – Big Top last night – available here'. Quite a number of people had gathered under the sign and were apparently ordering copies of my sermon.

I headed out, struggling with a rising feeling of self-congratulation. And then it happened. A guest blocked my pathway, waved a copy of one of my books under my nose, and asked if I would mind signing it for them. Ever seen that chap on the *Vicar of Dibley* who is an icon of glorious indecision? His catchphrase is 'No, no, no, no, no – yes!' I became that man. 'Autograph your book? Oh really? No, no, no, no, no – yes! Where do I sign? And what's your name? Shall I write a verse of scripture for you?'

For the rest of the day, I found myself unable to navigate my way around the site without being asked for my signature. At first, modesty insisted that I feel rather embarrassed about it, but before long, I found myself walking more slowly, just willing someone to pounce on me so that I could graciously bestow my signature upon them. It was getting to the point where I was feeling the need to have pen in hand, ever at the ready, so that I could more conveniently bless the ever-increasing members of my adoring public. I was famous! Hooray! This was really rather pleasant.

God has a way of puncturing our proud balloons in an instant – and I'm grateful that he exploded mine. Late in the afternoon, my right hand somewhat aching from scrawling a series of kind messages, I heard that voice again, that voice of God in my heart. And this time he asked yet another question, exocet-like in it's devastation, blowing my pathetic posturing apart in a second.

'So, famous in Butlins for a day, are we?'

Game, set and match to God.

I still sign books if people ask me to. And I'm enormously gratified and encouraged if someone tells me that something that I've said in print or preaching has been helpful to them in some way.

But the famous Christian syndrome is something to laugh about, and certainly not to take seriously. The mad joy that comes from knowing that more people know of your existence is a pathetic pursuit. I never wanted to be a large goldfish anyway.

ANGRY FROM CHICHESTER

I have just read a very angry, screamingly irate letter. It appeared on the letters page of our local city newspaper, together with a whole raft of similar 'Disgusted of Basingstoke' type epistles. The language in these missives is terse, sarcastic, and poisoned with bitterness. Clearly, there are a few people around here who are not at all happy. And the reason for their ire? The local town planners are considering granting planning permission to put a new façade and extension on a beautiful Georgian building that sits majestically at the heart of the city. There has been a flood of outraged protest.

I put the newspaper down, and I am angry too now, but it has nothing to do with proud buildings. I am angry at the face, the façade that has been placed upon the most exciting and supremely beautiful person in history. We the church, the guardians and key holders of the kingdom of God, have done something incredible. We have painted Jesus in boring colours. We have taken the Most Lovely and turned him into a wrinkled crone. This took great effort and ingenuity indeed.

Forget the gargantuan achievements of Everest mountain climbers and scrawny four-minute milers. Don't be impressed by the sleight of hand of David Copperfield, who can make a jumbo jet – or the Statue of Liberty – disappear into thin air. Stifle your gasp as you ponder the speed of our computers that are cutting-edge technology today and yesterday's metal junk tomorrow. These 'impossibilities' fade into nothing when compared with the 'accomplishment' of the Christian Church. Angels must be faint with shock as they consider what we have done.

We, the church, have made Jesus seem predictable and boring: a ho-hum deity who invokes little more than a yawn.

It has taken a long time, and a concerted effort, but somehow we have managed to take the author of colour and dance and variety, the master of spontaneity and humour, the one who calls himself 'The Life', and make him look like a domesticated, tame 'godlet' who may be vaguely admired, sentimentally remembered when troubles are rife, but who is bland, insipid and vague – an anaemic Galilean.

So how did we manage it? Perhaps we daubed him with the colour of irrelevance. We allowed him to become the extra-terrestrial baby in the manger, all white and pink: in a scene that is surely surreal. Mary, who for some reason chose to give birth while dressed from head to foot as a blue nun, sits serenely with a glowing goldfish bowl on her head. Dear old Joseph is not often to be seen, but when he is, he looks slightly nervous, as if he is concerned about the slightly wonky coffee table that he's just put together in the carpenter's shop. He doesn't usually have a goldfish bowl, but basks in the soft light of his virgin wife's halo.

Baby Jesus does, of course, have the goldfish bowl, and despite being only ten minutes old, is miraculously sitting up already, thanking the wise men and shepherds for being kind enough to come along to his little party. And the soft, moonlit hay is a carpet on which stand a collection of placid, grinning farmyard animals, who may only be sheep, but seemed to have a grasp of Old Testament prophesies concerning the birth of the Messiah, and are jolly glad to be in on the moment.

And what is it that the carol writer says of this bundle wrapped in swaddling cloths? 'And little Lord Jesus, no crying he makes . . .'

So, this baby doesn't cry then. Perhaps he wanted to but, instead, smiled at his mother with eyes that said 'I'd normally be crying now as I could do with a change of the old swaddling

cloths, but as I'm the son of God, and they're going to write a
song about this moment, then perhaps I won't'. Bunk! Of course
Jesus cried.

The popular portrayal of the nativity makes it all seem so
irrelevant. It is a scene from another world – a million miles from
the blood and guts and cold and disappointment and, 'Dear God
you arranged a virgin birth, but didn't you think to book us a
room?' type of feelings that may have flickered through the
virgin's mind when told that there was no room at the inn.

Stables stink: they are cold, damp stalls, where long shadows
drape themselves around the place to create a morose, dingy, half
light. Mice and rats fearlessly scamper to and fro, bold to the
threat of the stamping and snorting of great fat, grubby animals.
Dirty, bedraggled hay is scattered upon a soggy earth floor,
peppered with heaps of droppings. This is the 'glory' of it all,
Jesus, that you chose to come to our sweaty, squalid little world,
a King born in a shed. How much closer to us could you come,
and yet we call you irrelevant? And perhaps you are marked as
boring, because we do not allow too much room for you in the
church. Is that you I hear, knocking at the door of your own
house, Jesus? Are you just too unpredictable, too wild, too likely
to upset our middle-class apple carts? Is that why we, your
people, have often designed 'church' to be a well-honed mecha-
nism specifically engineered to keep you at a distance?

And what about the message that you said was *good* news?
Have we reduced the gospel call to a frozen, processed package,
a heavenly Good Friday agreement, which guarantees a pardon
from sin and a future in heaven? But isn't the gospel call far more
than 'four spiritual laws'? Isn't it a warm invitation to a life-long
friendship with Jesus, a Companion and Leader for the here and
now? How did we reduce a banquet invitation to being a
summons to a courtroom, a legal deal struck with the judge,
rather than a homecoming to a Dad who always has the barbecue
waiting?

Jesus, we have done it. We have turned the rainbow into mud.

We have turned the sun into a fluorescent tube. We have put a boring façade on you, the bright morning star.

Do I sound angry? I am. That's why I'm writing a letter about it. This is it.

TRADITION

ON BEING A SANDWICH FILLING

Today, I was a human sandwich filling. As a result, I now feel acute empathy towards tomatoes, because I now know exactly what a sandwich-bound tomato actually feels like, all sliced up and bleeding, shoved unceremoniously between the granary slices. Now I can extend genuine sympathy towards cheese, sliced turkey, and even Branston pickle. For I know what it is to be a sandwich filling.

The bench on Chichester railway station looked inviting. True, it was the precise epicentre of the most efficient wind tunnel, that is, Chichester station, but with ten minutes to wait for the train, I decided to take the weight off my feet. For some reason, I chose to sit in the middle of the bench. Mistake.

Within seconds, a slight, kindly looking elderly lady sat down on my left. I politely inched my bottom along a few inches to make more room for her. She looked a little frail, and quite nervous, and so I decided not to risk my normal 'good morning', but stole a quick look at her face. She shivered as the wind whipped along the freezing platform, but her eyes seemed warm. Deceptively warm. I was not to know that this woman was in fact the bottom part of the sandwich.

The other slice appeared a minute or two later. Another elderly lady sat down on my right. I slid my bottom back along to where it had been a few minutes earlier. She was ordinary enough, harmless even. I did not then know that she was to become the top slice, and as she muttered a curse about the icy wind, I could tell from her plummy accent that she was definitely an upper crust.

'What time is the London train?' she said, her high pitched jolly-hockey-sticks voice addressed to no one in particular, but apparently demanding a response from me. Her voice reminded me of a shrill headmistress from my junior school years, who demanded that I explain why I had inserted the sharp end of a compass into Binn Minor's left buttock.

'Er, I think it will be here in nine minutes', I replied, feeling, for some reason, like I was responsible for the chaos and confusion that is the British railway system. And then I added a fatal caveat, just four words that launched a festival of negativity: 'If it's on time'.

A sandwich was born. Upper Crust snorted with indignation, and immediately launched into a tirade, directed both to me, and to Lower Crust, about the abject horrors of her train journey the previous day. It was a predictable litany of woe: delays, filthy carriages, graffiti, and unhelpful staff. Apparently, the filthy toilets had been locked as well, so no one could use them. Inwardly, I considered the announcement that the guard might have made:

'We'd like to apologise to our passengers today, because as you know, the toilets on this train are locked. We regret the inconvenience caused by our locked conveniences, but I must point out that passengers leaving teeth marks on the toilet doors will be prosecuted. Connex South Central railways would respectfully advise passengers to cross their legs for the duration of this journey.'

I then began to ponder a deeper philosophical question. How did Upper Crust know that the toilets were filthy, if they were locked? Mmmmm . . .

My daydreaming was snapped to a sudden halt. Lower Crust spoke out now, her voice the lovely gorblimey cockney that revealed her roots in the East End of London. It was as if Upper Crust's indignation had pressed a button in her, releasing a flood of anger and grief. It was as if I was not there. She talked through my head to Upper Crust, complaining about the weather (always a reliable and favourite standby for complaining amongst the British); the local radio news (they didn't give accurate information out); the local bus station (I'm not sure what was wrong with it, but she was going to write to the council); the youth of today (fings ain't what they used to be); and the weather again. For the next eight minutes, I became the sandwich filling: the hapless centre of a symphony of negativity.

Let me switch the analogy. I was the net in the centre court at Wimbledon, and the two ladies shot wickedly rapid exchanges of complaint back and forth, oblivious to me, as the volleys whipped just across the top of my head, faster and faster now. Back and forth they went, the classes united now in a celebration of complaint. Their voices climbed an octave, their wrinkled necks shook and their Adam's apples danced an angry jig, as they moaned about – everything. I leaned forward, and placed my head in my hands, hands subtly placed over my ears. I couldn't move away; it would have been impolite and, in any case, my little comment had been the champagne that had launched their ship of complaints in the first place.

Finally the train came – on time. But even this did not silence their wrath. 'Would you believe it, a train on time, whatever next dear . . .' I fled to a smoking carriage – not to light up, because I don't – but I just figured that an atmosphere stained with cancer-carrying nicotine and tar was preferable to a whole train journey laced with the acid of negativity.

Complaining – it's the British national pastime. Forgive the stereotype, and there are always the notable exceptions, but sometimes the negative atmosphere that seems to pervade our Britishness hits me like a smog when I fly into Heathrow from America. Across the pond, our Yankee cousins seem quite happy to be happy. Critics will say that American culture is shot through with superficiality, but the Americans do, on the whole, seem to smile and laugh, and insist that I have a nice day. They ask me how I'm doing, and generally appear interested. They do seem really quite alive.

Contrast this with the fairly typical conversational style of we Brits:

'Hello. How are you?'

'Not too bad, thank you.' (Notice this – we don't advise the enquirer that we are in fact doing well, or that life is good. No, it's not too bad.)

'Things going alright with you then?'

'Yes, I really can't complain.' (Notice again the negativity in our positivity. We give the impression that we would really quite like to be able to complain, but unfortunately, there isn't anything on the immediate horizon to facilitate our having a good whinge. Never mind though – something worthy of complaint is surely just around the corner.)

Perhaps we need to take a leaf out of the Americans' book. And if that's too unpalatable to consider, then maybe we just need to take one out of the book that God inspired. For in those pages, he encourages us to be thankful: to practice a careful gratitude that refuses to take a single blessing of God for granted. We Christians should be constantly raising our glasses to toast the God who has decided to care about our humdrum lives. Gratitude is catching. Genuine thanksgiving is far more than a 'happy clappy' superficiality, or an 'I'm-a-fat-cat-and-I-got-the-cream' carelessness about others.

I didn't enjoy being a sandwich filling. I'd rather be surrounded by the thankful.

Call me insincere if you will, but . . . have a nice day!

REARRANGING THE FURNITURE

Looking back on it, I realise that it was a suicidal decision: foolhardy, crazy even. But I just had to do it. I was a driven man. I was nervous, scared, but something within me drove me to it. I took a deep breath, and stepped out like a Martin Luther marching resolutely towards the door of the Wittenburg Cathedral. Compelled by my convictions, I just did it. It was an historic Wednesday evening.

Wednesday night was the time when our church had its weekly Bible study and prayer meeting. As the senior pastor of the church, I led the meeting, announced the songs, and delivered the Bible study itself. But this particular Wednesday night was going to be an evening that no one in our church would ever forget. I arrived at the church building an hour before time, switched the lights on, and braced myself. I needed time and space in order to bring my extraordinary plan into being.

Flicking on the lights in the 'sanctuary', I paused for a moment. The hesitation almost paralysed me. Blood roared in my ears as I considered my wild plan. And then, as if steeled for the task by an invisible angel, I gritted my teeth, and just did it.

I did it! I rearranged the chairs.

For as long as I could remember, our small church had sat in pew-like rows every Wednesday night. There's nothing wrong with that at all, but I had been teaching that the church is a family, not just a study group, so it seemed to me that something a little more informal and relational would be more appropriate. And so I put the chairs into a big circle. There – it was done. And then I waited.

Thirty minutes later, the good people of our church began to arrive. The first couple were relatively new Christians. They had not had the benefit of the teaching that there was some kind of divine seating plan, and so with a smile and a cheery greeting, they sat down without comment. But it was the calm before the storm. A few of the 'more mature' believers began to drift in. Some just sat and went immediately into prayer, evidently determined to bring their concerns about the new circular arrangements to the throne of grace. Others were more immediately outspoken.

'Good evening Pastor.'

'Hello, how are you?'

'Fine, thank you, praise the Lord . . . errrrm, this is unusual . . .'

'What?'

'The chairs . . . they . . . er . . . they . . .'

'Yes?'

'Pastor . . . the chairs are in a circle!'

This was most observant, and so I congratulated the person for noticing the altered geometry of the chairs. But this, as you know already, was not actually their point. Their observation was a prelude to protest. And so it came. The first wave was based around historical precedent.

'Pastor . . . the chairs . . . we've just never had them in a circle before'.

'No, you're quite right, we haven't, which seems to me to be a perfectly good reason for trying something new.' I held the 'what kind of family sits in rows' argument like an ace card up my sleeve: a reserve weapon, in case the battle got bloody.

The next wave of attack was based around biblical instruction.

'Yes, but of course new doesn't necessarily mean good, now does it? Is it biblical to have the chairs in a circle?'

I wanted to laugh out loud at the idea of a God who would thunder commands about just how his people should sit them-selves down when they got together.

'I can't think of a single Bible verse in the New Testament that speaks about seating plans. Perhaps God doesn't care?'

And then, I confess, came a temptation to mischief.

'Actually, there is some New Testament help in the whole area of seating plans.'

The protester brightened up. Perhaps I was about to provide him with some unexpected ammunition.

'Paul preached for so long one night that a poor chap fell out of the window and had to have some serious prayer. Perhaps this teaches us to arrange the chairs, be they in circles or rows, at a sufficiently safe distance from nearby first floor windows. However, due to the fact that we are on the ground floor, this particular New Testament imperative is, in fact, not applicable to our situation.'

It was a naughty, but devastating blow. The would-be protestor sat down and assumed body language that quietly screamed 'oh God the chairs are in a circle whatever next?'

The next week, I decided to have another little reformation moment. We used to always have a cup of tea and a Rich Tea biscuit at the end of our meeting. I'd been thinking: why should we have it at the end? Why not in the middle? Were we actually sending a theological signal to our people by consigning the refreshment bit to the end of the meeting? Prayer is spiritual, Bible study is spiritual, sipping tea and biting biscuits is not quite spiritual.

The chairs were in a circle once again. People were actually getting to quite like the arrangement. We had our usual time of praise and worship, and then, on cue, everyone reached for their Bibles, like biblical gunfighters at the Okay Corral. Time to walk on water – or tea, as it turned out.

'Please put your Bibles down for a few minutes. We're going to have a cup of tea or coffee, and a biscuit or two. Rich Tea biscuits are not available this evening. Lets face it, Rich Tea means boring: only Christians eat them. McVities would go out of business if it were not for the huge quantities of Rich Tea biscuits that Christians chomp through every Sunday evening. So, I thought that we should splash out a bit – on Jaffa Cakes. I like the orangey bit in the middle. The kettle is boiling . . .'

There was a moment of stunned silence, as the awesome news settled in. To quote the carol writer, 'mighty dread had seized their troubled minds'. Tea? Now? Right slap-bang in the middle of the service? And not only that – but Jaffa Cakes as well? Oh, the madness of it all, the sheer decadence.

One spoke: 'You mean, we are going to have a cup of tea . . . now?'

I stood firm, fearless in 'we shall fight them on the beaches' spirit.

'Yes, we are.'

'In the middle of the service, we are going to have tea . . . and a biscuit?'

'Yes. Actually, there's no such thing in New Testament thinking as a service. If you asked old Paul if he had enjoyed the 'service', he wouldn't know what you were on about. In the early church, they had no services – but lots of meetings. Meetings together to eat and drink and pray and cry and strengthen one another. The very concept of a 'service' is difficult to present from the pages of the New Testament. So, put the kettle on, and let's get biblical.'

And so we sat there, our chairs in a circle, sipping our tea, savouring the luxuriously lovely orangey bits, and had a very nice time.

I take my hat off in respect to the members of the church that I was leading. It seems so small, so insignificant, but on those two Wednesday evenings, we embraced a little bit of change. We asked questions about why we do what we do, and came up with what seemed then to be some risky conclusions as a result. I'm glad that we put the chairs in a circle and put the kettle on.

There's a heart-warming postscript to this story. Years after the circles and biscuits episodes, I decided to tell a Big Top audience at Spring Harvest about our little adventure into change.

A man who had been dragged along to Spring Harvest by his believing wife was watching television in his chalet. He didn't particularly want to be at the event, had gone along for a quiet life, and was certainly not a Christian. He was flicking through the channels looking for something interesting, and inadvertently came upon the live broadcast from the Big Top. A chap was speaking and for some reason was talking about Rich Tea biscuits and Jaffa Cakes. Intrigued, the man decided not to change the channel. What kind of event was this that his wife had dragged him to? Was he the unwilling guest at a biscuit appreciation convention?

He watched the rest of the broadcast, and listened to me as I presented the gospel. And – you've guessed it: that night he surrendered his life to Jesus, and became one of God's followers and friends, and all because his interest was caught by my story of Jaffa Cakes and Rich Tea.

He's been back to Spring Harvest every year since, as an enthusiastic believer, serving as a steward. The stewards work enormously hard, policing the venues, moving chairs, serving communion. They are easily spotted, as they wear very bright tabards – orangey tabards.

TRADITIONALISM

Tradition is a word that has been vilified in recent years. The suggestion from some quarters is that anything that was must be out dated, antique and religious: only the brand new, the allegedly creative, and the apparently innovative counts as being significant. The trouble with this is that we end up spitting on history and rejecting out of hand perfectly good practice, simply because it's been around for a while, and inventing new traditions to replace old ones.

But tradition can be dangerous – so Jesus taught. Reserving his most withering language for the religious experts of the day, he announced with blistering insight that they nullified the word of God with their traditions. It is the mindless, unthinking traditionalism, which refuses to allow the new wine of the Spirit to flow, that causes the problem, not the use of the well-worn, and sometimes even archaic, practice itself.

I quite enjoy ceremonial tradition, even if it's a bit mindless. If the lawyers in the House of Lord's want to perch themselves on a woolsack because wool used to be England's primary commodity, then that's fine by me. And I quite enjoy the State Opening of Parliament, when the Queen is kind enough to deliver a speech that she never composed in the first place. The summoning of the Members of Parliament is a hilarious little routine. Black Rod, a dark, forbidding chap who could easily be mistaken for a medieval cross-dresser, knocks on the door of the Commons, which is opened, and then ceremonially slammed into his face, poor chap. Resolute to the end, he knocks again, and summons the Members to hear Her Majesty's speech. It's a harmless piece of theatre, just like the 'dragging the Speaker to the Chair'. Apparently, history records that many of the Speakers of the House lost their jobs by losing their heads, literally, and so it's supposed to be a job that one accepts with great reluctance: hence, the members 'drag' the successful candidate to the Speaker's chair. At best it's colourful pomp, and helps bring large consignments of American tourists into the country, and at worst it seems like a bunch of public school types continuing their 'ragging in the dorm' behaviour, and hoping that Matron won't catch them.

I have discovered myself to be a traditionalist of the more mindless variety. Every morning, I begin my day by inserting my contact lenses into my eyes. I have a careful little ceremony worked out for this intricate and delicate procedure. Wash hands, open container, and *always* put the left lens in first, followed, obviously, by the right lens. The other day, I made a horrifying departure from the established norm. I am ashamed to confess that I placed the right lens into my right eye first, and was about to follow this deft move with the placement of the left lens to the left eye, when I realised that I had made a terrible, terrible mistake. This was not the way to do things! Whatever next? Standards were slipping. And so I am embarrassed to confess that I removed the right lens and placed it back into its sterile holder. I then placed the left lens onto my eye, as the ceremony properly demanded, and then inserted the right lens back in again, locating it on my right eye for the second time that morning. And as I concluded the procedure, it suddenly occurred to me that I might need to seek psychiatric assistance.

Why do we have traditions anyway? Some of them are simply formed by habit, the well-trodden pathways that result from repetitive walking. Others serve as a link to history and destiny: reminders echoing from yesteryear about who we are and where we have come from. But sometimes tradition is more sinister, because it is forged out of preference and control. We like things the way they are in *our* church, conveniently forgetting that Christ died to redeem *his* church, and it's *his* preferences concerning *his* bride that really matter. And then we hide behind the threadbare scenery of tradition in order to control and manipulate what will happen.

It was the late David Watson who was told by one lady, 'We don't want any of that supernatural Christianity in *our* church, thank you very much'. Control was the temptation both of Pharisees and disciples. The former were blinded to the wonder of a stinking Lazarus staggering alive out of his tomb, because the miracle was too inconvenient, too out of their control. Jesus was breaking their self-claimed monopoly on things spiritual, and such an enemy of their control must himself be controlled: even by tying, and nailing hands to the cross. But those would-be friends and followers of Jesus often wanted to tidy things up around him. Having a crowd of fussing mothers and snotty-nosed children clamouring for a hug and a blessing just didn't fit in with the agenda. Wasn't Jesus discussing important stuff, like divorce, with the religious luminaries of the day? And so they tried to shoo the mother and toddler group away – and in so doing, ignited a terrifying outbreak of anger from Jesus.

And Peter, such a friend of Jesus, had to learn how not to be a control freak. Don't go to Jerusalem, Jesus, you'll only die there. Don't think I'll deny you Jesus: I'm stronger and bigger than that. Only the thrice crowing of the rooster silenced Peter's control-freak tendencies and brought him, finally, to his knees.

So let's not throw out everything that has some history in the name of innovation. But beware, lest you try to handcuff the hands of God with that old 'we don't do it that way around here' routine.

CANA

Picture the scene. It had been a perfect day. A radiantly beautiful bride, warm candlelight dancing in her eyes; a beaming, mildly embarrassed groom, all broad smiles and nervous laughter; the careless, happy chatter of children dashing here and there, while the musicians excelled themselves.

And then disaster struck, bringing the threat of shame in a culture where hospitality was of the greatest importance. The frantic mutters of servants, urgent behind cupped hands said it all. The easy flow of wine suddenly, abruptly halted: all gone now. The whole day now threatened by miscalculation, or budget, or unexpected guests drinking their fill.

A hasty discussion in the corner, an exchange between a woman and her son, and servants are sent off, commanded to fill huge stone jars with water. Moments later, with appropriate pomp and ceremony, the jars are carried in, and eager guests hurry to taste their host's late offering. The wine is exquisite, testimony surely to the host's outrageous generosity: not for him the well-worn practice of waiting until your guests were past caring about the quality of their drinks and then serving the cheapest plonk.

The host is both glad and mystified. Gladness crowns his day, as his friends and family raise their glasses and toast his gift of hospitality, yet he is mystified because he had been carefully watching the level of pitchers, and had been dismayed to see them drop so quickly. Anxiety had gnawed away at the pit of his stomach throughout the afternoon, stealing his joy. He was peering into the abyss of family disgrace, and now, he is the talk of the town! But where had the best vintage come from?

At a corner table, a woman sits, a bright smile written all over her face. Next to her, a young man sits quietly, his eyes alive with joy.

Put aside your familiarity with the Cana wedding story for a few seconds. Imagine that a major Christian ministry is planning a special launch event. Perhaps there would be an array of dark-suited evangelical dignitaries in solemn attendance. Readings would be recited with careful enunciation. Theologically rich prayers of commissioning and blessing would echo around the rafters. A sober air would pervade this auspicious occasion.

But you chose to begin your ministry at a party, Jesus. A place where wine tumblers were raised and music filled the air, where children chased each other around the room, and where the bride danced with her man, shy anticipation in her eyes.

And, horrors, you didn't just attend ('only there to be a witness, you know'), but you provided the wine, and good stuff it was too. And it gets worse. The wine you gave was the end of the evening supply; just when disappointment was beginning to take hold because the pitchers were running low, you provided the means for the party to continue late into the night. Whatever next, Jesus?

The truth is, you don't belong in a religious box at all, Jesus. Perhaps that's why so many of us love you.

SEX

BEAN THERE, DONE THAT

I have an ambition. I'd like to be good at life. I'd like to be able to negotiate the hairpin bends of existence on planet earth with smooth, accomplished control. I don't want to live out my days stumbling and bumbling from one embarrassing episode to another with the finesse of an evangelical 'Mr Bean'. But it doesn't seem to happen. When it comes to life, I feel like a bloke with a provisional licence that's due to expire in the year 2040.

I displayed my life 'learner plates' again just the other day, following a wonderful Christian wedding. Christians can become very animated and excited when a wedding is in the offing. Perhaps it's the recognition that for the happy couple, sex is about to become a divinely endorsed option, hence the sense of party in the air. And some boisterous partying goes on. I once attended a 'stag' night and was delighted to witness a well-respected Christian leader having a large frozen trout inserted down the front of his trousers. Both he and the trout had my sympathies, but it was fun to participate in some harmless laddish behaviour. The night before my own wedding, I had attended a memorial service. Not a single fish, frozen or otherwise, in sight there.

It seems that the more 'holy' (and sometimes legalistic) the group is, the more outrageous the pre-nuptial events seem to become. I attended a Pentecostal wedding recently and was astonished to note that the blushing bride had been presented with a vast range of 'dodgy' accessories, which were probably not purchased at the local Christian bookshop. These included some edible underwear (presumably an emergency snack in case one gets peckish on honeymoon), pasta that had been moulded into, shall we just say, the most unusual forms, and a novelty condom which discretion forces me to describe simply as . . . a novelty condom. Unfortunately, someone slipped the aforementioned rubber item into my computer bag. Bad idea!

Yesterday I was speaking in Salt Lake City, Utah, and, having delivered my sermon, was walking to the car, accompanied by a lady who serves as the church administrator. I had decided to change my flight and get a hotel at the airport, and she had agreed to help me with the arrangements. She asked for my air tickets, and I reached down into my bag, scurrying around for the passport wallet. The first thing that came out in my hand was a corkscrew. I believe that one should always be prepared for the possibility of a decent bottle of wine, and so I always keep a corkscrew in my bag. Here I am in Salt Lake City, Utah, which is what our American cousins call a 'dry country'. That means one cannot purchase alcohol there, it is a city-wide equivalent of a bishop's birthday. And here am I, guest preacher, brandishing a corkscrew. I dropped it like a hot coal back into the bag, and tried to produce my very best *'oh my goodness how did that get in there and who does it belong to anyway?'* look. Hopefully Ms Church Secretary hadn't noticed my mobile wine-bibbing tool. But it was to get worse . . .

I carried on chatting while scurrying around in the bag and, not concentrating, I plucked out a package that I assumed would be a packet of mints. Animated now in my verbal flow, I waved it around in my hand to emphasis a now long-forgotten point. The dear lady looked nervous. Perhaps she was allergic to Polos. I glanced at what I held in my hand, and was grateful that I hadn't opened the 'mints' and popped one in my mouth. They would have been decidedly chewy, seeing as they were . . . condoms.

My heart sank, and my mind raced and, once again, another hot coal hit the bottom of my bag. But I knew that the damage had been done. Surely an explanation was required.

'You, er, probably noticed that I pulled out a packet of condoms just then', I ventured, terror-stricken, and proceeded to tell her how they had come into my possession. She laughed a little too loud, and then, having got myself out of that mess, I dug another hole.

'So then, do you think you'll be able to get us a motel room?' I spluttered, unthinkingly using the term *us* instead of *me*.

Excellent! I could imagine her telling the story. The guest preacher produced a corkscrew, a novelty condom, and asked about getting a motel room. Party on down, dude. This could be the end of me.

The moral of this absolutely true story? There is none. I just thought that you'd enjoy the outrageous stupidity of yours truly. I wish that this story was just a myth, a figment of my hyperactive imagination. Sadly, the truth of it testifies to my own capacity to be a one hundred per cent proof idiot. If God can use brainless me, he can surely use anybody . . .

And the church secretary that I inadvertently invited to a party? She's still laughing.

NO SEX, PLEASE, WE'RE CHRISTIANS

You are given the choice between passionate sex and a nice chocolate digestive biscuit – select one now. Such was the embarrassing dilemma experienced by an evangelist friend of mine. He and his wife were 'overnighting' at the in-laws and, due to bed shortage, were sleeping on the lounge floor. All was fine until they foolishly decided to risk a session of blissful lovemaking. It was early Saturday morning, and they mistakenly assumed that the rest of the household was still asleep. Wrong!

All was going rather well until the father-in-law helpfully decided to make an unannounced entrance mid-coitus with a tray of tea. Unfortunately, they were at a point of irreversible commitment in the proceedings, and so the hapless dad stood there stunned and frozen to the spot, while the earth moved before his eyes. Ten seconds later, when the fireworks had finally diminished, dad put the obvious question: 'Would you like a biscuit with your tea?'

And, according to my friend, nothing more was ever said about the incident. Like most of us, who don't want to concede that our parents have ever had sex, even to create us, this father-in-law/turbo caterer preferred to pretend that the episode had never happened.

When I became a Christian, the church seemed to be involved in a similar conspiracy of silence about sex. It wasn't that sex was frowned upon, it's just that no one acknowledged its existence. I remember looking at a visiting minister during a rather boring sermon one Sunday morning, and wondered how he had managed to acquire his children. His wife was the church organist and she wore a huge sun-eclipsing hat. Irreverent questions rushed through my mind. Did they make love? Did they enjoy it? Did she take her hat off when they did?

Once a year we would have the obligatory hearty chat on sex from the youth leader – a jolly chap – but you really needed a gift of interpretation and a map reference to know what he was on about. The message was implied, but clear: good married people probably do have sex, but they do so mainly to make babies, and they are much more interested in reading the Bible 3.2 times per week than they are in earthly passion. Perhaps this was a distant hangover from the medieval Church's doctrine that the Holy Spirit would depart from the marital bedroom during intercourse, and then return immediately when it was all over.

'Was it good for you darling?'

'Yes, but don't mention it . . . *he's* back.'

It wasn't all bad. There was a refreshing lack of 'nudge nudge' innuendo in our conversation. It was a joy to breathe clean air. Of course, that also meant that there was a fair amount of naiveté, and I wondered sometimes what visitors to our church made of our innocence. Like the day when the worship leader stood up and declared, 'Come along then, ladies, let me have my way among you.' I am sure that some of the older folks probably thought that 'Carnal Knowledge' was a new board game from Waddingtons.

All of this led me to have a slightly suspicious attitude towards sex. As I approached marriage, I subconsciously put sex in the same category as golf – likely to be good fun if you got it right, embarrassing if you didn't, but not really spiritual.

And so the wedding night arrived. Kay and I drove off to our honeymoon cottage armed to the teeth with a copy of *The Act of Marriage*, the most shocking and radical manual available for bright young Christian things like us (two positions listed, the missionary and the missionary reversed). Despite the fact that we didn't finally get to the cottage until 3 a.m. in the morning, I insisted that we have an extended Bible study and prayer time (and the prayer was not, 'for what we are about to receive . . .') before retiring. We then got up at 8 a.m. the next morning and went to a nearby church, where I was invited to testify to the blessing of God upon my newly married life to about forty-five grinning communicants. We had tea with the minister, and then went back to church in the evening. Our honeymoon was filled with passionate, lusty – hymn singing. It's as if we felt that we needed to sanctify our faltering steps into the land of Eros by breaking the Guinness World Record for church attendance.

All of which causes me to sigh with relief when I hear sex being talked about freely and openly in the church twenty years later. I'm delighted that Christian couples these days can get decent pre-marital counselling which includes extensive discussions about KY jelly and condoms, and follow-up chats after the honeymoon, to see how everything went. It's not unusual for people who prepare folks for marriage in our church to get a call from a honeymooning couple asking for some quick advice – and why not? But more than clarity, education and openness are needed. We also desperately need a positive antidote to the total unreality about sex that is portrayed in tabloids such as the *Sun* and *Sunday Sport*: which market the idea that Britain is reverberating with supremely athletic bodies all enjoying super-sex every night. It's just not true!

The *Big Issue* reported a glorious story of sexual reality recently. Evidently, an unfortunate Brazilian chap called Carlo Paia purchased himself some surgical assistance in the form of a strategically placed erectile implant. But all did not go as planned. The supposedly ingenious device kicked into instant action whenever anyone in his house turned on an item of household electrical equipment. The poor chap found himself in agonising difficulties when his wife switched on the kitchen blender to make a milkshake. The blender was hastily turned off, and peace and tranquillity were restored for a while, until Mr

Paia's mobile phone rang, with the same disastrous result. The only thing to do was to turn off the electricity in the house altogether – but even this didn't solve the problem. Mr Paia lamented, 'One minute I was sitting in the dark with a bag of ice on my lap, then suddenly the next door neighbours switched on their TV to watch *Wheel of Fortune*, and my trousers exploded'.

Anyone for a chocolate biscuit?

RELATIONSHIPS

HOORAY FOR SUE!

'I am really offended!'

If I had a pound coin for every time I've heard a Christian use the 'O' word, I'd weigh a ton. Some believers have a fantastic capacity to be offended. They are the ones everyone else in the church describes as 'prickly', 'sensitive', 'awkward', or 'difficult'. You can always hear the crunch crunch of eggshells being walked on when people get around them. It doesn't take much to irritate them. I met four 'black belt' offended types recently. They were older ladies, and they were so upset with me, that they stomped out of the Sunday evening church meeting, before I'd even started preaching. I had noticed that, five rows back, there was a lot of muttering, sniffing, narrowing of eyes, and then finally the march of the haughty four. So why the quadruple walkout? I later learned that my sin was that I had invited the congregation to take a few pre-sermon moments to say hello to each other. Apparently, this particular church didn't include the saying of hello in its vision statement, hence the huffy puffy walkout. The pastor was a warm-hearted, compassionate shepherd, who was eager to visit the retiring sisters to restore them as lost sheep to the flock. I admire him. I was inclined towards a lamb kebab with heaps of mint sauce. Easily offended people bore me.

Sue is a lady that I bumped into recently, who could have so easily have chosen the offended look: you know, pouting lip, downcast eyes, and woundedness bleeding from every pore. But she didn't go that way. She chose to laugh instead.

Sue was walking into our Sunday morning meeting in Chichester. I was in a hurry and didn't pay any attention to the fact that she was pushing something in front of her as she navigated her way through the oaken double doors. Sue had been pregnant: hugely pregnant. So massive had she become during the past nine months that it was rumoured that Goodyear was sponsoring her confinement. Hurrying in behind her, I glanced, momentarily, at what seemed to be her still considerable girth and the words tumbled out before my brain had time to catch them.

'So then Sue, no baby yet?'

She paused in the doorway, obviously stunned by my rank stupidity.

'Actually Jeff, I had the baby this week. That's why I'm pushing this pram, believe it or not'. Her eyes sparkled with the joy that breaks out when one meets a truly, authentically, stupid person like me. But there was no malice or edge in her voice.

'I'm so sorry Sue . . . I mean, er, congratulations, it's just that you still look, so, er . . .'

'Big' said Sue, completing my hapless sentence. I frantically searched for some ground of the swallow-me-up-now variety.

'Well, er . . . sorry . . . well done anyway! He's beautiful!' I gushed; praying to God as I did that the bundle before me was a male.

Sue could have been irritated, galled, or just mildly upset by my stupidity – but she was the reverse. She laughed with me, not at me. And the next time I saw her at church, she asked if I was doing okay. 'I nearly telephoned you that afternoon,' she smiled. 'I was worried that you might have been concerned. You didn't have to be at all.' She could have glared, but she grinned. She gave grace in the face of my mindlessness. Her hobbies don't include being offended.

Hooray for Sue!

SORRY!

The man in the seat next to me on the aeroplane was chewing tobacco and spitting the juice in a cup. I'm a tolerant enough person, but as another shot of yellow stained saliva hit the polystyrene, it occurred to me that this practice should be considered a capital offence, preferably involving hanging, drawing and quartering – and thumbscrews.

I groaned.

My spitting fellow passenger was also very, very gay. His voice was the high-pitched, effeminate giggle of caricature. Either that, or he had attended an infant school where Liberace was on the teaching staff. I groaned again – a deep, masculine groan this time.

There was a pause, and the polystyrene spittoon received momentary relief. He spoke, apparently to me. We had not been introduced.

'First time in Denver?'

My mind raced with twenty replies, which included a lengthy statement about the fact that I have never found the male physique to be remotely attractive, that I love my wife, that I do not have a homophobic bone in my body, would never dream of dancing to 'YMCA', no, I'd been to Denver before, and I'd never enjoyed Boy George's music that much.

'No, I've been to Denver before', I smiled – not too warmly. 'But I often fly into Colorado Springs via Denver.'

He spat again, forcefully this time. I had apparently said something very wrong. His nostrils flared and his eyes blazed. He explained that he hated Colorado Springs, because it was full of right-wing Christian conservatives, who were sworn, vocal enemies of his lifestyle. I looked frantically with one eye for an emergency exit. This man was totally unaware that he was sitting right next to a Christian, and a leader at that. This could get tricky.

I listened with gathering alarm as he told me how he had been 'de-baptised': a private ritual of his, designed to ceremonially renounce any allegiance to God and church. Catholicism, he continued, had been shoved down his neck from birth. And then came the question I was dreading.

'So. What do you do for a living?'

I coughed nervously and considered lying, but couldn't think of an occupation.

'I'm . . . a minister. Of the Christian kind.'

A long pause from him. Narrowing eyes. Pursed lips. At last he spoke.

'Minister, eh? You would probably line up with the right-wing conservative crowd.'

Again, my brain raced and I mentally bumped into potential sermonettes about Jesus loving sinners and hating sin, texts from the book of Romans, warning comments about AIDS and death and hell. I honestly couldn't think of what to say.

And so I just quietly explained why I followed Jesus. I said that Jesus had some radical things to say to all of us about sexuality – and not just homosexuality. But most of all, I apologised. I wanted this man to know that I felt shame about television evangelists who rant and rave and pick on certain types of sinners. I apologised because I felt that, too often, the church railed against the gay community rather than reaching out to them. I said sorry.

His eyes widened, and I thought that they were going to fill with tears. But he smiled a great warm smile, and put his hands together, prayer like.

'Jeff, I thank you for your words: I am humbled by them. And please know that I can see that Jesus Christ is at the centre of your being. Once again, I thank you.'

And then, remarkably, our friendship began. He scribbled his address down, and asked if Kay and I would join him for dinner in Denver. And three days later, he came to our hotel, and delivered complimentary tickets for our whole family for the Colorado Rockies' baseball game. Suspicion and enmity were sent packing by a simple expression of heartfelt regret. And in a few days, Kay and I will be in Denver for a dinner appointment. And it all started with . . . sorry.

ENOUGH SAID

The conference had been going rather well – my address on the opening evening had been well received. There was a spring in my step as I skipped down the hotel stairs, two at a time, heading towards the crowded lobby. Just time for a coffee before the first session of the day. Suddenly, a voice rang out from the landing above. Two ladies, delegates from the conference, had spotted me and decided to brighten my morning with a word of encouragement, which is always welcome. Their choice of words, however, caused quite a stir in the lobby.

'Jeff . . . heeeellooo . . . wait!'

I paused on the last stair, and looked up. They leaned over the stairwell, faces beaming, eyes bright with kindness.

'Jeff . . . both of us just wanted to say . . . thanks SO MUCH for last night . . . '

The teeming lobby instantly joined me in my pause, and looked at my reddening face with interest.

'You were ABSOLUTELY FANTASTIC last night . . .'

The lobby wrestled with moral outrage and veiled admiration.

'Yes, we both agree – we haven't laughed so much in years.'

I attempted a response of thanks but due to acute embarrassment, a high-pitched sound, like that of a chicken being strangled, emerged from my throat. Head down, I rushed out of the crowded lobby, avoiding the eyes of the other guests, some of whom clearly wanted me executed as a moral reprobate, and others who wanted to slap me heartily on the back and ask my

118

secret. Of course, at one level, the exchange was rather refreshing in its naivety and simple purity, uncluttered by innuendo. I don't miss all that tiresome 'nudge nudge, wink wink' chatter from my pre-Christian days. But the other side of the story is that these delightful ladies, in their hurry to be kind, hadn't paused to consider their words – and their effect on the crowd in the lobby.

Something similar happened a few weeks ago at a major event that happens in the Spring when they're bringing the Harvest in. A lovely older lady rushed up to me after a seminar.

'I enjoyed that seminar, Jeff. Will you be speaking tonight?'

I replied in the negative. No, Steve Chalke would be speaking that evening.

'Oooooh, even better!' replied my erstwhile fan.

And as 'even better' emerged from her lips, her eyes screamed with alarm, as if she knew that her choice of words weren't the best: as if she was reaching frantically to catch them before they came tumbling out of her mouth . . . aaahh, too late.

I can't tell you how many times I wished that I had paused, just for one tiny second, before blurting out my thoughts. 'Slow to speak' is the biblical description of the Christian who engages the brain before releasing the mouth. A few seconds of deliberation and thought can save hours of recrimination and regret.

I conclude, therefore, with a formal apology to the lady that I met while on a hospital visit. She was visiting the same person as I, and smiled as I introduced myself. 'You must be the patient's mother,' I declared confidently, shaking her hand. The warm smile vanished, to be replaced by an icy glare big enough to sink the Titanic. 'No . . . I am her sister.'

Enough said.

THE ANONYMOUS LETTER

The anonymous letter is a frequently used communication technique, believe it or not, in some churches. Disgruntled and offended parishioners express their irritations to pastors and leaders by dispatching an unsigned epistle. The lack of signature and, therefore, the hidden identity of the writer, gives them the 'Dutch courage' needed to put the most toxic poison on paper. Scurrilous accusations, inferences and innuendoes jostle with each other in the grubby scrawl. The net effect on the recipient is devastating: it's like being hit by a relational exocet that comes screaming in from the dark, demolishing in a few seconds your confidence, your sense of calling, and hope.

Sadly, it's not a new idea. The famous evangelist D L Moody received such a poisonous pen letter while actually preaching a sermon. Someone out there in the congregation was apparently feeling highly uncomfortable, and so, hastily scratched out a note, and passed it back to an usher, who calmly walked up to the pulpit. The folded note had Mr Moody's name written on it, reasoned the hapless usher, so Mr Moody should receive the note, immediately. Moody took the note, unfolded it carefully, and read its brief content.

One word was written on the page: 'Fool'.

Moody sighed, re-folded the note, and made an announcement.

'I've just been sent a most unusual letter from one of you in the congregation', he said to a fairly shocked crowd.

'Now this is most interesting. I'm often sent letters where

people write the body of the letter, but just omit their name. On this occasion, in writing the single word 'fool' the person concerned has omitted to write the letter itself, and has only signed their name'. He then proceeded with his sermon.

I saw the power of the anonymous letter while Kay and I were working on the staff of a church in Oregon. Having been a well-received part of the team for some eighteen months, we had felt that it was time to move on into a wider ministry of itinerant Bible teaching. An announcement was made to the church, advising them of our resignation and imminent departure. 'The letter' was sent to the senior minister and all of the deacons, but of course, Kay and I were not sent a copy by the anonymous writer. The letter alleged that the senior minister was jealous of the warm welcome that Kay and I had been shown, was nervous that we were popular, and so had acted to force us to leave. We were, the letter declared with the authority of one that knew, being driven out of town. The senior minister felt a high level of anxiety at this scandalous, and totally untrue, suggestion. I asked him to allow me to deal with the problem in my own way.

It was our final Sunday in the church, my leaving service, and I was preaching my last sermon. The place was packed. Time for some redemptive fun.

'Before I conclude, I want to let you know that the senior minister and the deacons of this church have each been sent a copy of a letter, a letter without signature, which accuses them of treating Kay and me badly, and suggesting that we are, and I quote, 'being driven out of town'.

I paused. Tension crackled in the air. I look round at John, the senior minister, who shifted from side to side on his seat on the platform. I continued.

'I have decided to tell you the unedited truth about the senior minister of this church and the deacons too. Hey, it's my last Sunday here, and I have nothing to lose – I currently have the microphone in hand – so why don't I just go ahead and spill the beans, as it were, on these people . . .'

The level of tension rose even higher. I decided to milk the moment. I walked back away from the pulpit and stood beside John. Placing my hand on his shoulder, I said, 'Let me just tell you the unbridled truth about this man. Again, what have I got to lose now? Let's go for broke.'

John looked up at me with pleading eyes, sweat breaking out now on his forehead. I had to wrap this up, if only to put poor John out of his misery.

'This man has done nothing – and I say again, nothing – but bless, shower kindness, encouragement, and help upon me, my family, and my ministry. He and the deacons of this church have done absolutely everything in their power to help resource and release me. I owe them a great debt. And so, to whomever it was that wrote the anonymous letter suggesting some kind of ridiculous conspiracy, I would like to say two things. First, check your facts, because you couldn't be more wrong. And second, next time you sit down to put pen to paper, have the moral courage to sign your name at the bottom of the letter. An unsigned letter is not worthy of the time needed to read it. It is a work of cowardice. Whoever wrote it, please hear me say this loud and clear: you need to repent.'

I sat down, and the congregation rose to their feet in what was, not a standing ovation for me, but a message of love and endorsement for John and the team of deacons that served with him. I looked at the crowd whooping, yelling, and waving their Bibles, and realised that someone, somewhere out there in the crowd, was the author of the anonymous letter.

A FRIEND IN NEED

It was a dark day in every sense. The hospital staff had thoughtfully dimmed the lights of the small, private ward where my father lay dying. The fluorescent glare was banished: replaced by a softer, warmer lamp – a light to die in. I had rushed into the hospital, summoned by the stark words that say so much: 'you had better come right away'.

My mother sat by his side, dabbing her eyes, holding his hand, whispering reassurances. This was the scene that I had imagined for months, during long nights where sleep eluded me. It was not my father's death that I feared: I knew that he had made his peace with God. After years of silent anger against heaven, the result of a lost youth spent in Italian and German prisoner-of-war camps, and the sights and sounds that had been his daily existence through those long years, he had come to terms with the news that there was a God who cared for him.

During a long, hot summer in America, Dad had finally invited Jesus to take charge of his life. That evening, he came with me on a preaching engagement in central Oregon. I remember the joy of pointing up into the balcony, and announcing to the congregation, 'This is my dad. He became a Christian today.' They clapped and cheered, and stamped their feet, and he stood up and waved like a member of the royal family. It was a happy day.

And then the stroke had hijacked his brain, and robbed him of the ability to speak. He had become a silent prisoner of his own body: fully coherent and intelligent, but sentenced to the moment

123

by moment frustration of being utterly unable to communicate, except by grunts and hand signals. It was a cruel fate for a man whose favourite thing in life was conversation, but like the prison sentence of his youth, he bore the solitary confinement with brave dignity.

The final blow came when they told us that he was dying of emphysema, where fluid gradually fills the lungs. It was this that had robbed me of sleep. I begged God to allow my father to die in peace. This man had suffered two long prison terms: to die a drowning man was an agony too great to contemplate.

Dad was in a morphine-induced coma, and I knew the moment that I saw him that it would not be long. The nurses, so pressurised and busy, were so consistently caring and kind. They did their best to make him comfortable.

My mother went out for a well earned few minutes of fresh air, and I sat quietly with my father's hand in mine. And then I remembered one very special evening, a couple of years earlier.

Something remarkable happened when I was staying at my parents' for the night. I was tucked up in bed – it was past eleven – when there was a knock at the bedroom door. The incomprehensible murmuring outside the door told me that it was Dad: even though the stroke robbed him of his speech, he never stopped trying. I invited him to come on in, but wondered – what could he possibly want? It was late in the evening, and we couldn't have any kind of conversation, so what was bringing him into my room now?

I will never forget the moment when Dad came to the side of my bed, knelt down, and then slowly and carefully took the blankets and the sheets and tucked me in, just like he had when I was tiny. He brushed a stray hair away from my forehead, kissed me on the cheek, and was gone. He could not speak, but he dramatically expressed his loving care for me that night. I remember lying there for a long time, a man with almost grown children of my own, feeling warm, safe, and loved.

And now, conscious that my dad was struggling, just hours

from death, I felt that it was time to return the compliment. I will never know if he understood, but I whispered in his ear: 'Dad, it's Jeff. I love you so much. Soon you're going to be with Jesus, Dad. It may feel bad now, but you're safe, Dad. I'm going to tuck you in.' I took the hospital blanket and the crisp white sheet, and tucked it into the underside of the mattress. I hope dad knew.

A couple of hours later, it was time for him to leave. My dad was always a joker, loved to laugh, and kept us guessing in death as well. The nurse, searching for a pulse, could find none. 'He's gone', she declared, solemnly but warmly. 'No he's not, he's back. . . . *Now* he's gone . . . no, he's back.'

She waited a minute or two, unwilling to take us on the emotional rollercoaster any longer. Finally, she spoke again.

'Yes, he has gone now'. And this time he had.

Mum and I both burst into tears. As I leaned over to kiss my dad's still warm forehead, the telephone at his bedside rang. Who could it be?

The nurse answered the phone, and announced that it was someone wanting to speak to me. A Dr Chris Edwardson from America was on the line.

Chris and Jeanne Edwardson are our closest friends. Our families have holidayed together for years: Chris is my closest confidante. I took the phone.

'Jeff, it's Chris. Look, I'm in Canada and I'm driving right now, but God spoke to me and told me that I should track you down because you needed me to call right now. What's going on?'

I told my friend that Dad had died less than thirty seconds earlier, and that I was right beside him now.

'That's why the Lord asked me to call you, Jeff. I'm your friend, and I love you. Your dad is with Jesus now. I'm praying for you, and Jeanne and I will be over to be with you in the next few days.'

I put the phone down, and marvelled. There was I, at one of the most poignant moments of my life. Many times, I had quizzed Chris about my dad's likely death, with the challenge of the emphysema. And now, as a gift of grace from God, he had called from the other side of the world at the precise moment that I needed him.

I had tucked my dad in. And now, a similar warmth and security came, as I realised the incredible blessing of genuine friendship.

God is kind.

DEATH

FROM HERE TO ETERNITY

The ageing car was a rust bucket, apparently held together by fading bumper stickers. 'My Boss Is A Jewish Carpenter', announced one. I pondered the thought that the Saviour from Nazareth was currently at the right hand of the Father, busily churning out coffee tables at knockdown prices. An even older sticker encouraged fellow motorists to 'Honk If You Love Jesus', while another gently warned would-be honkers to 'Be Patient, God Isn't Finished With Me Yet'.

Still another sticker declared 'I've Had A Faith Lift'. Was this car driven by a Christian plastic surgeon with a lisp? And then, the most helpful sticker, 'In The Event Of The Rapture This Car Will Be Without a Driver'. Helpful advice this, for those who believe in that particular interpretation of Scripture. Those left behind after the Second Coming may be scratching their heads trying to work out why millions of people had suddenly disappeared from the planet, but at least they wouldn't be left wondering why that car was driverless. Mmmm.

A familiar stirring of irritation surfaced somewhere inside my head, wrinkling my brow and nudging me to mutter a superior comment about pie-in-the-sky space cadet Christians, as I urged my own stickerless car past the slogan-bound rustmobile. It was the same frustration that had sparked a few days earlier when I drove by a church building in Tulsa, Oklahoma. If the Southern States of America are the Bible Belt, then Tulsa is the belt buckle. Thousands of churches litter the streets of the sweltering city, and most of them have huge billboards outside. One had particularly frustrated me. The city had been through a heatwave and a large number of people had died of heat exhaustion. This church put up a sign saying: 'If you think it's hot here, then just wait . . . '.

'So much for good news', I murmured with measured superiority, and then treated my fellow family members to yet another sermonette denouncing Christians who are so heavenly minded that they're of no earthly use. I had quietly chuckled when I saw an eminently non-Christian sticker with the words 'Jesus is coming – look busy'.

I admit it. I get weary of Christians who seem to think that the next exciting event in God's diary is heaven. But then, just last week I went to Redding, California, met Paul and Margaret, a couple who have heaven in the hearts. Their car, like mine, is stickerless. We were riding together in this cliché-free vehicle when I asked an innocent question, more for the sake of polite conversation really. 'How many children do you have?'

Margaret hesitated, as if she were not sure of the number of her own offspring. There was a lengthy silence, and I was tempted to make a 'witty' comment about moving on to an easier question, but something told me to be quiet. Something was right.

'Well Jeff, we have three children, but one of them is with Jesus. Our eldest daughter was murdered by her boyfriend when she was nineteen. He beat her up, threw her from his truck and then ran over her. So, yes, we have three children: two on earth and one who is with Christ.'

I stammered and searched frantically for words that could form a response to such an awful tragedy, but Paul and Margaret neither needed nor demanded my little contribution. In the next hour or two, they allowed me to peer into the cavern of their pain. Paul sat clutching a coffee cup in one hand, a photograph of his beautiful firstborn girl in the other. They told me that you never, ever recover from such a trauma. They told me that you slowly learn to smile again. But most of all, with their laughter and their tears and their sparkling hope-filled eyes, they made me realise that part of them was already living in the not yet of forever. They had been to hell and back, and had tasted heaven in the journey. They were not ethereal, spacey or clichéd. But they were living as citizens of a kingdom that will never end, and looking forward to the reunion party.

Little things don't bother them anymore. As church leaders, they aren't too concerned about bowing down to religious culture. Margaret, a minister's wife, had a nose ring, just because she wanted to. And she was planning to get herself a tattoo as well. 'I just love to stir up those religious devils', she smiled, not the smug grin of arrogance, but the settled joy of one who has looked death itself in the face and found out that there's someone bigger, who quit carpentry to become a King. After I left them, I felt that, in some way, I had been ushered into an audience with greatness. And I was deeply challenged. Has my Christianity become so focused in the here and now that I have lost sight of the wonderful forever that lies just beyond time's horizon? The old Southern slaves had looked for a sweet chariot to swing low, coming for to carry them home. They had nothing in the now, and everything in the not yet. They were temporary paupers, groaning for their inheritance. They were going from here to eternity.

Paul and Margaret don't have stickers: they have deep, bloody wounds. But one day they will dance again without a limp, arm in arm with their daughter, spinning and jumping with the Jesus who stands above death and hell.

You've heard it a thousand times, but stop once again and consider this: as a Christian, you're going to be with Christ – always. That's forever. No wonder they call it good news.

A BIG, BIG HOUSE . . .

Jory was a bright, cheeky, twelve-year-old with an infectious giggle and a razor-sharp wit. He was a young man who had decided that he liked life a lot, had decided to live as a follower and friend of Jesus, and now was seriously enjoying the journey. John and Cheri, Jory's parents, were and are good friends of mine. I have often stayed in their home in Colorado Springs, and found it to be a true haven of love and laughter.

I remember speaking at a youth meeting in Jory's home town. I was feeling rather ancient, and so, in a fairly pathetic attempt to try to be just a little bit trendy, I had donned my orange 'Tommy Hilfiger' fleece sweater. Jory ambled up to me as I walked in, took one look at my ambitiously fluorescent attire, winked, and said 'nice try, Jeff'.

Jory loved music. I can remember one particular song, obviously about heaven, that seemed to be playing endlessly in his room:

> There's a big, big house,
> With lots and lots of room
> There's a big, big table
> With lots and lots of food
> A big, big yard, where we can play football
> A big, big house,
> That's my Father's house . . .

Jory and Justin, his elder brother, were staying at their grand-parents' home in Wisconsin. Wanting to fetch chewing gum, and some sunglasses to shield his eyes from the late afternoon sun, Jory had hopped on a four wheel motorised bike and had headed back to the house, crossing a quiet road as he did. Mission accomplished, he hopped on the bike again to head back across the field to rejoin his brother. But it was not to be.

He probably never even saw the truck that ploughed into him, carrying him and the bike some yards up the road in a moment. Grandpa, hearing the sound of screeching tyres, rushed out to discover his beloved grandson obviously dead on the road. The distraught truck driver stood by, his hands wringing with grief.

And now, a couple of days later, Kay and I were at the most emotional breakfast gathering. John and Cheri, their eyes swollen red with too many hours of sobbing, were just three hours away from an occasion that no parent should ever attend – the funeral of their youngest son.

We had received a telephone call just hours earlier, asking us if we could fly out to be with John and Cheri, and asking me to be one of the speakers at the funeral service. We sat through the long flight with increasing dread – what words could we possibly say to these dear friends of ours who were now at the very extremities of pain? How could we comfort without resorting to cliché?

Now, the four of us, together with two other close friends, joined at a table of tears to talk through the last minute details of the funeral service, and to try to help prepare the parents for this potential ordeal. We talked songs, the order of things and who should speak when and where, and then, during a lull in the conversation, John leaned over to ask Kay a question – an enquiry that sent a surge of panic racing through me.

'Kay, has the Lord said anything to you about Jory's death?'

It seemed like a question too risky to answer. To say that God had said something, only to be mistaken, could cause enormous wounding at such a painful, sensitive moment. The danger of sounding clichéd was looming. I looked down at my coffee, and hoped that Kay would calmly and gently affirm that, no, she had not heard from God, and yes, she knew that God would be faithful and ultimately speak into this valley of tears. Except that she didn't answer in the negative.

'Yes John, I do believe that God spoke to me this morning . . .'

I scrutinised the coffee even more closely. It was very black. I held my breath and tried to kick Kay under the table. I missed.

'I feel that God impressed me to tell you that Jory really is dancing with the angels now . . .'

The black sheen of the coffee reflected my stare. 'Dancing with the angels now'. Did this not sound a little trite? Apparently not.

Dabbing his eyes with a tissue, John calmly responded.

'Kay, I know that you're not aware of this, but Jory loved to dance – it was what he liked doing best. He couldn't keep still when there was music playing. But there's something more significant. Yesterday, Cheri and I went into the funeral home to say our goodbyes to Jory. When the time came for us to leave, I looked at the face of my son for one last time, leaned over the coffin, kissed his cheek, and my parting, final words to him as a father were, 'dance, Jory, dance.'

The rest of our breakfast together was a buffet of laughter and weeping, of sensing that God had spoken and would yet speak, and yet sensing the swirling fogs of mystery, and the ever looming question 'why', that so frequently comes calling when we find ourselves in the season of tragedy.

There are so many things that I just can't figure out, about God, about life, and about the nature of suffering. But I know this: there is a bright, laughing-eyed young man called Jory who is partying right now in the Father's house; eating at a big, big table . . . and maybe kicking a football around as well.

MY VERY FIRST FUNERAL

I knew that they knew, by the way that they tried to stifle grins, and whispered behind cupped hands into each other ears. Undertakers are not supposed to smile, even furtively. But they couldn't resist it. They knew that the young minister was a funereal virgin. This was my very first time. I had never seen a corpse before, and I was scared to death.

I had spent a long, sleepless night, tossing and turning and dreaming brief dreams about coffins and corpses before waking for the umpteenth time, my forehead beaded with sweat. I was scared of my fear: would I faint at the sight of the body? I knew that my very first funeral was going to feature an open-topped coffin (that sounds like a convertible sports car). And so the body would not be hidden away, safe and sound, in its brass handled container. No, this first funeral was going to include a very open casket, containing one very dead person. I was mortified.

I knocked at the door of the house where the funeral party was being held, half expecting the deceased to answer the door. Taking a big deep breath, I jumped into the hallway, alarming the mourners who obviously thought that the minister was either armed and dangerous, or had been watching too many James Bond movies.

The coffin had still not arrived, and so my over-anxious entrance was in vain. I smiled lamely, and said something that I hoped soundly vaguely sensible. The funeral director smiled back.

At last, his colleagues arrived with the dearly departed. I thought that I was going to scream as they set the trestles up and

135

placed the coffin upon them, right next to the sausage rolls and gherkins, which had been provided for the post-burial bash. Slowly, so slowly, they unscrewed the lid, and I decided to take microscopic interest in one of the gherkins as they inched the lid open. Gherkin in hand, I turned slowly to view the corpse – and immediately knew that all was going to be alright. His face was a chalky, powdery white, his eyes clamped tight shut in the long sleep of death, his hands folded together across his chest, prayer-like, a fitting final posture for this belated man of God.

The relatives came in, fussed around and picked up thin slices of pizza and told each other how very nice he looked; how very lifelike he looked. And then they asked me for a photograph. I assumed that they just wanted a snap of me, as the officiating minister at the funeral, and so I swallowed the last piece of gherkin, with which I had been so well acquainted. But I was mistaken. They wanted me to be in a photograph together with the departed brother. I couldn't believe it at first. Surely not, I mean, how was such a photograph to be taken? Should I get down beside the coffin and nestle in closely, head to head, as if the deceased and I were out for a night on the town together? Should I put a friendly arm around the coffin head? And should I smile for the camera? After all, my fellow photographic model was – dead.

They said that a smile would be fine, as the dearly departed had indeed gone elsewhere and was now with Jesus. So why not smile, they reasoned. I agreed, put my arm around the coffin as if the deceased and I were posing for a post-football snapshot, and did my best to look happy. I hadn't planned on getting that close to the body. Perhaps it was morbid fascination, but I studied the texture and lines of the face closely. The stillness, the utter absence of life was fascinating to behold. The flashbulb did it's work, and minutes later, I was being shown a Polaroid snapshot of myself and a very cold, dead person. I remarked that it was a good photo – but inwardly wanted to say 'he doesn't look well, does he?' It didn't seem appropriate.

It was time to go to the cemetery, so they screwed the coffin lid on again, and we began our slow drive to the leafy park. But there, again, another unusual experience awaited me: this family was determined to bury their dead. I had expected to do the 'ashes to ashes' bit, and then walk away, and allow the gravediggers to do their work after the mourners had left. But this family had a tradition of acting as gravediggers themselves. The women sang beautiful spirituals, their lilting voices a mixture of lament and celebration as they sang about the 'sweet by and by'. And as they harmonised together, the men took up shovels and spades and filled the grave with earth. Great clods of rain-soaked earth thudded onto the coffin lid, and within minutes, the wooden casket had disappeared from view. Still they sang on, until the grave was quite filled, and a mound of earth rose above ground and the lilies had been arranged delicately. Then, and only then, did any mourner attempt to leave.

Back at the wake, there was laughter and tears, and eating and drinking. In a quieter moment, I wondered about the way these people treated death: the open coffin, and the photograph, which would be sent to relatives overseas and the insistence from the family that they literally buried their dead.

Did they do this because they were unafraid to stare death in the face? Did it help their mourning to make sure that any sense of unreality was shredded by the brutality of deadness? Our culture so often disguises death – to speak of it is 'morbid'. We hide our undertaker's shops down back streets, and use just about any turn of phrase as a cosmetic to cover up the harsh reality. A person is deceased, departed, gone on before, on the other side: anything but . . . dead.

My first funeral taught me far more than I had expected. I had bumped into a group of Christians who were able to stare down 'the last enemy' – death itself. Their confidence was not based in some sentimental 'it'll be alright on the night' view of heaven, but anchored in the sure hope that comes from the Jesus who has wrestled death and won the fight for all of us who will believe.

Death is very dead.

PRAYER AND PROPHECY

LET US PRAY?

There are a few announcements that tend to make my palms sweat and my heart skip a beat. That nervous, panicky feeling rushes upon me when my friendly dentist kindly advises me that what he is about to do is going to hurt – just a little. Horrendous agony, guaranteed to tip me into the abyss of insanity is just around the corner. An entire toolbox of fiendish, cold, stainless steel instruments of torture is about to be dumped in my mouth, helpfully subsidised by the National Health Service.

Similar nervousness breaks out when an aeroplane pilot announces that there is a 'slight problem'. Actually, the cockpit has fallen off. Nigel the pilot (they're all called Nigel) and his crew members have already landed. We, the passengers, have not yet landed. Tough!

And my stomach flutters when the worship leader beams an enthusiastic grin and says in a high-pitched voice, 'Let's have an extended time of worship, shall we?' We will now warble our way through three hundred overhead transparencies, many of which are utterly illegible. These transparencies are mysteriously stacked out of order and will only be actually displayed during the singing of the last verse, at which time the second verse will be displayed. We will 'feel led' to sing each of these songs at least twice through. Even if we do not feel so led, we will sing the songs. Even if our Lord Jesus interrupts the proceedings with his long awaited Second Coming during the worship time, we will still sing those three hundred songs.

But as a speaker with a national ministry, (I think the definition of 'national ministry' is that you go up the M1 at least four times a year), there is another jaunty little announcement that is guaranteed to cause some trembling in the Lucas boots. It goes like this:

'We'd like to get a few people together to pray for you before the service, Jeff.'

Help. Dial 999. Call the Samaritans. Agony cometh. Oh yes, it all sounds so very innocent, even kind, and definitely *very* spiritual. But I feel a flutter of concern when I am told that I am going to be prayed over before a meeting – and I am not alone. Many of my fellow itinerants, themselves executive club members of the Granada Services Loyalty Programme, share my terror of the pre-meeting prayer gathering – a terror which is increased a hundred-fold if the word, 'intercessor' is casually mentioned. This means that the spiritual storm troopers are being brought in, the 'no-God-isn't-deaf-but-he-isn't-nervous-either *In Jeeeesus Name!* brigade'. Much volume, foot stamping, flag waving and tambourine chewing ensues on these occasions. My friend Adrian Plass often tries to escape these pre-meeting prayer times by hiding in the toilet. It's a sad, pathetic sight, to see one of the best Christian writers in the world, hiding in the cubicle, trying to handcuff himself to the cistern.

Some are wondering why such anguish is caused by these well-meant gatherings for prayer. Why is it that Plass sprints to the loo, and I sometimes would rather have my toenails extracted than be prayed for before meetings? Lest you be concerned, let me say immediately that it is not because I am cynical and unbelieving. I am convinced of the value and power of prayer. And I have absolutely no doubt about the sincerity and spirituality of those who gather to pray. Actually, I really am glad that people are taking the time and energy to call upon God to move. So why the pre-meeting prayer allergy?

First of all, these gatherings can be quite physical. Most Christians are nice enough, but the practice of prayer gives them the perfect excuse to spit in your ears, face and generally pebbledash your Bible with saliva during a time of high octane intercessory fervency, which is quite frustrating, especially if you've showered before the meeting.

And then there's the joy of being the centre of a circle of praying warriors, some of whom have gently placed their hands upon your shoulders. Others, who feel inclined to massage your back, rub your shoulders and neck (which can be quite pleasurable, but it's unseemly to moan with pleasure during intercession), and still others who like to place their hands on one's chest, stomach, knees and feet. The use of anointing oil exaggerates the terror even more. I once emerged from a prayer gathering with my suit jacket mottled with greasy thumbprints: enduring souvenirs of an over-enthusiastic prayer time.

There is also the problem of predictability. Less physical prayers stay on the outskirts of the circle, often springing up and down on their toes during prayer and telling God what his name is. Often there is great concern that no one member of the trinity might feel left out of the occasion. 'Oh, Father, we really just pray Jesus, that you, Jesus, God, Lord, Holy Spirit, Father, will come, Jesus, Father . . .' Others find it helpful to head-butt tambourines or walk around the room, punching the walls, which are innocent of any crime. Code phrases are often used on these occasions. For example, the employment of the biblical quotation: 'We just thank you that where two or three are gathered together in your name, there you are in the midst', normally means, 'We're not expecting too many people to show up tonight, God, but your presence would, nonetheless, be most helpful'. Another code phrase is: 'We just really thank you that if one person, just *one* person, becomes a Christian tonight, then it will have all been worthwhile.' Interpretation: 'No one has become a Christian around here for forty-five years, and we've blown the entire evangelism budget for the decade on tonight's little bash, so a result of some sort would be nice'. Every denominational group, most certainly including my own, has it's own jargon, but sometimes I long for a little more down to earth reality in prayer.

Another problem is that these gatherings can actually be quite anti-social. It's bad form to arrive at an event during the pre-meeting prayer time. As a fully paid-up member of the human race, I often feel the need to nod, smile, or even do something like mutter 'hello', when I meet people for the first time. Don't even try this with a group of pre-meeting pray-ers. They will often respond to your nod or wave with a determined blank look – an 'excuse-me-don't-you-know-I-am-conversing-with-him-above' expression.

I often feel nervous about knowing how to behave during these prayer times. A few days ago, I was artistically arranging my book table so that God's people could fulfil the will of God for their lives in the purchase of fine Christian literature. The event organiser came over, smiling, lulling me into a false sense of security. 'So then Jeff, lets be having you, we'd like to pray before we start.'

The organiser saw the flicker of anguish in my eyes at the mention of the prayer bit, and pressed the case home.

'We really *insist*, Jeff. We are waiting. Come'.

Like a lamb led to the slaughter, I followed this intercessory Schwartzenegger into the little room at the back, where a group of very lovely people were engaged in reminding God that he needed to show up. The group were kind enough to gather round me, and I placed my hands together, fingers pointed upward under my chin, in the thoughtful contemplative stance that I often adopt for these occasions (another helpful posture, particularly in renewal meetings, is the open hands 'fill my cup' outstretched position). But on this occasion, the 'praying hands' method seemed right. All was going swimmingly until I suddenly got an itch in my thigh, and quickly snapped my right hand down to scratch it discreetly. Unfortunately, I failed to realise that the aforementioned event leader had placed her hands out towards me, and as my arm snapped down thigh-ward I chopped her arm, karate style, in the process. She cried out in pain. I felt very embarrassed, and mumbled an apology, but this was drowned out by the pray-ers, who assumed that the dear sister was experiencing a Holy Spirit manifestation. Two or three people stepped to her side murmuring 'More, Lord'. (Don't ever have a heart attack in a pre-meeting prayer gathering. You could be thrashing around the carpet frantically trying to suck some air into your lungs, while God's gathered people wave their arms around, grin in delight, and ask God to give you more.)

But for me, the biggest problem about being prayed for is the pressure that often comes packaged with the prayer. Despite disclaiming comments like 'Oh God, you know we just want Jeff to totally relax and be himself tonight' (which tempt me to look up and say 'Okay, if that's the case, right now I'm not sure if there is a God – so does anyone else fancy preaching?'), often the pre-meeting prayer brings a back-breaking shed load of expectation.

I often turn up for meetings quite filled with faith and genuinely have a sense that God is going to be at work – and then feel the tonnage of the hopes and fears of the prayer group.

'Oh God, no pressure, but we are aware that Fred is bringing his Auntie Mabel tonight. Thou knowest, O Lord (but we shall nonetheless remind you), that Auntie Mabel is a chicken-sacrificing Satanist with only fifteen minutes to live, and that this is, therefore, the very last Christian meeting that she will attend. So, put the words in Jeff's mouth that will convict her, save her, heal her, and turn her into a Malaysian missionary by this time next week. And may the blind see, the deaf hear, the dead rise up – but no pressure, Lord.'

I listen with sinking heart, feeling now a rising sense of in-adequacy. I consider my sermon, which seemed so inspiring and incisive when I wrote it, and now seems to be about as inspiring as the mortgage deed on my house. And the prayer for healing reminds me that I have a headache. Having prayed that the Lord would remove the dull thud in my forehead, I have just taken two aspirin, without water. The tablets have left a powdery taste in my mouth, a reminder on my taste buds about my limited success in the area of healing. Raise the dead? Not tonight, I think . . .

And so, as the saying goes, let us pray. But let's not spray, make speeches, or shovel an inordinate weight of pressure upon the poor unfortunate who happens to be delivering the talk. And as we pray, let's ask the Lord for the padlock combination. Someone needs to unchain Plass from that cistern.

HITCHHIKING ANGELS AND
FLINTSTONE GIFTS . . .

Back in the Seventies, Abba, those glitter-sprayed Swedes who staggered around on platform heels tall enough to induce airsickness, warbled that they believed in angels. I believed in angels too. After all, they flew frequently through the pages of my Bible. But I struggled with the stories of angelic appearances that frequently did the Charismatic rounds. It bothered me that most of the angel population apparently spent a lot of their time hitch-hiking up and down Britain's motorways. Apparently, angels particularly enjoyed coming to the aid of stranded Christian motorists. The winged messengers would often use the break-down as an opportunity to announce that national revival was on the way, even though the hapless motorist was probably more interested in an assurance that the *RAC* man was on the way.

Surely, I mused, a lot of angel sweat could be spared by the inclusion of an *RAC* application form into every *Journey Into Life*. The angels would thus avoid unnecessary grease and could get on with doing something important, like protecting me. But I never revealed any of these concerns when I heard those stories. I really, really wanted to believe them. I was hungry for the endorsement to my fledgling faith that the stories brought. But deep down, I wondered . . .

A similar agnosticism would seize my heart some Sunday mornings 'in church', particularly when the time came for the weekly spot of speaking in tongues and the ensuing 'inter-pretation'. I heartily *believed* in the reality of both gifts, but I wasn't so sure about the versions that we received with clockwork regularity, just before the bread and wine were dished out, and usually from the same dear old chap. 'Ya-bee, ya-boo, yea, ya-boo', he would cry with feeling. On one occasion I think that our Lord actually said 'Yaba daba doo' to his gathered people. Everything in me wanted to jump to my feet and yell out 'Wilma!?' But instead, sitting there, seven rows back, I pushed my head deeper into my hands, and muttered an earnest prayer of thanks for the privilege of hearing God speak.

But somewhere deep inside, I wondered whether this was the real thing or just a nice and undeniably sincere chap getting excited about God, and not much more than that. The 'interpretation' didn't help out much either: it usually involved the Author of the Universe reminding us that (a) he liked us a lot (b) he was likely to come back at any moment and (c) we had better sort ourselves out jolly quick because it might well be tonight, particularly if we were planning to go to the cinema. I really *wanted* to believe it was real – after all, everybody else did. There was a silent peer pressure to go along with it – no one ever actually *talked* about the Flintstone gifts – they were just there, just God. Okay?

Sometimes I feel the same way about our talk of revival. Before you pick up that stone in order to heartily cast it Lucasward, let me quickly say that I *am* convinced that God is very much on the move in Britain right now. I want to believe with the believers, hang out with the hopeful, and run from the cynics and the critics who seem to delight in telling us that our God is doing nothing. But I don't want to get caught up in a revival rhetoric, where, in our excitement and eagerness, we rush to declare that revival is here, and then overstate the significance and importance of the things that we ourselves are involved in. Our relationships are important at this time and can help us to find the way forward. Rather than being swept mindlessly along, we need to be able to challenge, provoke, and ask the difficult questions of one another.

'Do not put out the Spirit's fire', and 'do not treat prophecies with contempt', Paul the Apostle writes, encouraging a healthy respect and openness to the gifts of the Spirit. But he also encourages them to 'Test everything' and 'hold onto the good'. Real revival can certainly survive the cut and thrust of honest debate and dialogue, which is vital. How else can we put these things to the test?

And, by the way, I *do* believe in angels. I had an encounter with one in Cork, Ireland, a few weeks ago. But that's another story . . .

THE 'MOUTH IN GEAR, BRAIN IN NEUTRAL' OFFICIAL AWARD

I have travelled a lot of miles and met a lot of very strange Christians. Some of them are on a mission from God to offend as many people as possible. They target speakers, and I've learned to spot them from a distance. Waiting around long after the meeting has finished, they shift uncomfortably from one foot to another, biding their time, waiting their moment. They rarely look you in the eye, and frequently preface their verbal missile with a comment like, 'Now I want to speak the truth in love brother . . .' Whenever someone tells me they are going to love me with the truth, I look around for the nearest nuclear shelter.

Some of them are just plain rude. Like the lady who came up to me after I'd preached and asked: 'Excuse me, have you ever had a stroke?' I affirmed that I had never, to my knowledge, suffered from such a debilitating event and asked why she should venture such a question.

'Well, it's because, when you smile, only one side of your face goes up'. I was desperate to tell her that I was just seriously ugly, and ask what excuse she had for her own facial arrangement, but instead I smiled and said, 'Er . . . God bless you', and hurried away.

I smiled and similarly blessed the man who asked me what it was like living in England during the Second World War. And the woman who asked me why I was wearing a hairstyle that looked like something out of the *Texas Chain Saw Massacre*. And the other man, who just had to come and confess to me that he had hated, loathed and despised me for years, and just felt much better for getting it off his chest. I was so pleased for him.

But I want to present my 'Mouth in Gear, Brain in Neutral' award to a chap that I met a few weeks ago in America. I flew out there to speak at a men's retreat. It was, as they say, quite a remarkable time. Thirty men made decisions to become Christians. Three hundred thousand dollars were pledged in giving, to local churches and mission. Malc Garda led worship that was raw and powerful: the anointing of God was tangible. And then, at the end of one of the most amazing meetings of my life, a man marched purposefully across the room and sat down at my side. I looked him up and down. He was smartly dressed and looked normal enough, but in the following few seconds, his words literally took my breath away.

'I . . . I have something to share with you that I don't really want to say', he stammered nervously.

I quickly looked around for a nuclear shelter, but there was none, so I told him to say his piece. And he did.

'When you were speaking this morning Jeff, I noticed something terrible. You see . . . I saw a mark on your forehead . . . it was the mark of the beast'.

What do you say to a man who wanders over for a friendly chat and quietly mentions that he believes you to be one of Satan's secret agents? I was dumbfounded. I didn't know whether to laugh, slap him or run my head through the nearest Visa machine.

'And what is that supposed to mean?' I ventured, hopelessly. 'I know what it means,' he replied solemnly, and, noticing the bewilderment in my eyes, he quickly added, 'but I love you brother.'

Oh goody! He tells me I've got a 666 bar code on my head and then wants to sing 'Bind Us Together' with the antichrist.

I searched for words, but there were none. Looking back on it, I can laugh now, but right then, it felt like a knife had been plunged between my ribs. I decided to put the 'God bless you' routine aside for once. I asked the man to go away. And he did.

And I went on my way, wishing that Christians who are

tempted to speak what they see as the truth in love might consider
stopping, thinking, waiting a while, thinking again, praying, praying
again, and then – perhaps – saying their piece. Or as the Bible
says, 'Be quick to listen, slow to speak'.

Got something that you're just dying to say? Slow up a little,
then life – and not death – will be the result of your words.

And if you own a portable nuclear shelter . . . would you
consider loaning it?

Note

Anecdotes used in this chapter have been taken from my book,
Gideon: Power from Weakness, Kingsway Publications, 1999.
Used by permission.

A FOOL

I was excited as I hurried into the meeting. The worship band was serving a pre-meeting cocktail of high-energy worship/rock and roll/thrash. There was a sense of high anticipation in the air. Just under a thousand leaders had gathered for four freezing days at 'Stalag Luft 7' (not its real name), a windswept holiday camp on the blustering east coast of England. Inspiration for this entertainment resort had been surely gained from the epic film *Colditz*. After twenty-four hours, I had considered forming an escape committee.

I had been trying quite hard to enjoy the conference, but the truth is my heart wasn't really in it. The draughty event came during a period of heavy soul-searching in my own life. I was asking some fairly significant and serious questions about my own identity and calling. Crisis is too strong a word to describe my condition, but I was feeling confused, discouraged, and not a little battle weary. The issue centred on my commitment to humour in teaching and preaching. I like and indeed love laughter, and am very nervous when I get around Christians whose facial arrangement suggests that they are wrestling with severe constipation. I bump into far too many believers who feel that laughter is okay, as long as it is planned as a post-death experience in the eternal bliss of the afterlife. I'm not prepared to wait that long for a giggle, and love to employ humour as a genuine communication technique. I don't tell jokes – punchlines are too risky – but use stories (some of which are shared in this book) to illustrate and provoke, to entertain and create interest. Not a month goes by without someone likening me to a Ben Elton, and I'm very flattered with the comparison. Elton is a very astute craftsman; not only in his communication technique, but also in his sharp ability to be an observer in the zoo we call life.

While there are quite a few people who seem to like what I do, there are inevitably those who feel that I'm just a superficial lightweight who lives for the next funny story. There is a feeling abroad in Christian circles that the really heavyweight and helpful brand of preaching and teaching is 'deep'. But sometimes we say that preaching is 'deep' when what we really mean is, 'I didn't understand a word of that, did you?' I remember once sitting through a numbingly boring meeting where Buddhism had seemed attractive. The preacher chose to speak on the zippy subject of 'Rudolph Bultman and the Quest for the Historical Jesus'. He had dreamed up this very natty and tantalising title for his message, which was displayed on the overhead projector. Not only was his theme utterly inappropriate for what was a Sunday morning family communion service, but also, he managed to deliver his content in a totally incomprehensible way.

'So what did you think of that sermon?' I asked a good friend, as we left the meeting hall.

'Well, Jeff, I didn't understand it at all, but I think it was good preaching.'

I was tempted to eat my Bible there and then. How can it be good, if no one understands it? How can communication be profound, if 98% of the hearers haven't received the communication? Let me put it subtly: such a suggestion is bunk. Switch analogies for a moment:

'It doesn't actually start, and the steering wheel is missing, but I do believe that it's a good car'

'People want to kill themselves when she opens her mouth, but the Lord has given her a wonderful gift of singing.'

'I believe him to be a fine piano player. When he sits down to perform, it sounds like a sack of spanners being thrown down the stairs, but he is good nonetheless.'

And so I believe that my commitment to simple preaching to adults – which children can understand and enjoy – and truth delivered with a smile is a legitimate one. But the suggestion that I am a 'lightweight' was chafing me somewhat. I had complained to God about it. Please don't gain the impression from what follows that God and I sit around all day having matey little chats. I, like everyone else, find it difficult to work out if God is speaking to me, if Satan is talking, if I'm talking to myself, or if the revelation in my head comes as a result of overindulgence in a curry the night before. But I went to God with my complaint anyway.

'So God, have you called me to be a fool for your sake?'

The answer that seemed to come back was not, shall we say, lengthy and reasoned in its argument.

'Yes.'

'A fool for Christ. Great! Thank you God. Why can't I be an evangelical statesman who is respected for the profundity of his exegesis?' I shared my sense of being called 'a fool' with no one.

And now I'm sitting in the meeting, the worship team is wrapping up, and I'm conscious that it is quite possible that God is about to talk to me through one of his, and my, friends.

Gerald Coates had advised me that he had a prophetic word 'brewing' for me, and that he was planning to give it that night during the public meeting. This could be good news or bad news, and filled me with both hope and dread. I took my seat and waited. I was hoping for a 'good' prophecy – you know the sort – blessing, anointing, and possibly the provision of a new car. I wasn't at all prepared for what came next.

Gerald called me onto the platform. The musicians played quiet 'wallpaper-backing-music-for-prophetic-bits' melodies. Gerald held a microphone in one hand, but in the other, he held what looked like a multi-coloured piece of cloth. I speculated wildly. Perhaps he was going to say that I was a spiritual Joseph with an amazing technicolour dreamcoat? Was I going to prison?

Was I going to be flirted with by a Pharaoh's wife? Was I going to get a baker into serious trouble?

None of the above was the case. He unfolded the cloth – which turned out to be a jester's hat, complete with loud, harlequin colours and bells. And to my horror, he placed the hat unceremoniously upon my head. The music played. I turned and faced the crowd, fearing that I now looked utterly ridiculous. My suspicions were confirmed. People in the crowd initially sat quietly, trying to look serious, after all, this was the prophetic bit. But the sight of me so garbed soon began to tickle a collective funny bone, and within seconds people were, first sniggering furtively, and then laughing out loud. One or two were punching one another, heads thrown back and shoulders shaking with mirth. I turned away, my face flushed beetroot red. I was angry with the laughing congregation, and angrier with Gerald. What was he playing at, subjecting me to such public humiliation? What was God doing? Didn't he know that I had experienced enough dismissive sarcasm from fellow Christians to last me for eternity? My anger was transformed in just a second as Gerald began to prophesy:

'You have been willing to be a fool for Christ.'

Help! I had told no one that I had felt that God had told me that I was a fool . . . this was so accurate, it was spooky.

Gerald talked and prophesied about how the fool, the jester, was so valuable to a King, and then told me that he felt that God was saying that it was vital for me to know two things. Firstly, I would be highly criticised: more so than any other leader present that night. God would give me grace and strength, but barrages of criticism were on the way. Secondly, I needed to learn a greater level of dependence upon God. I needed to lean on him every day, specifically and consciously. And then he produced a beautifully carved wooden bishop's staff. The staff had been given to Roger Ellis. Originally belonging to the Rt Revd Trevor Huddlestone, the fearless campaigner against apartheid in South Africa, it had ended up through a series of circumstances, in Roger's hands.

Gerald took it from Roger, and now handed it to me. It was not his to give, but he's like that . . .

'You should carry this wherever you go in ministry, as a reminder to you to lean hard on Jesus everyday. You will wish sometimes that I had never prophesied this. It will be an inconvenience to you, it will delay you at airports, some will misunderstand your carrying it in the first place.'

Then he prayed, and I don't really remember much more. Suffice it to say that God's strength and power came to an odd-looking chap with a multi-coloured fool's hat, clutching a bishop's staff.

And so, for two years I carried the wonderful, wretched thing with me wherever I preached. Some understood, and some laughed. A helpful chap at Spring Harvest suggested that I might like to have a lapel pin of a bishop's staff made so that I wouldn't have to cart the furniture around. Customs officers and immigration officers love to come up with wholly original gags at my expense.

Immigration person: 'Oh that's a big staff you've got – are you going to hit me with it?'

Me: (grinning broadly) 'No, it's an antique you know . . .'

(And I think with a snarl: 'No, but I would very much like to hit you with it, you brainless twit. Oh that's a big mouth you've got. Are you going to swallow me with it?')

The staff gets in my way. It's always the last thing to come out when I claim my luggage at airports. It gets lost on aeroplanes – have you ever tried filing a lost baggage report for a bishop's staff? And the size of the thing is awkward. I climbed onto a train with it and inadvertently poked a fellow passenger in the head. I apologised profusely, and he looked both bruised and bemused. What could I say?

'Sorry to have whacked you, but please know that this is a prophetic accessory that I am carrying.'

But it has done exactly what Gerald suggested it would do. It serves as an irritating, intrusive reminder that every day I need God.

An airline finally lost the staff for good a while back. I still have the head of the staff, but the pole was lost on a transatlantic flight. And so, for now at least, I no longer carry the staff. But I do carry a sense of dignity about my calling to be a jester for the King. And I'm still learning the reality of leaning on Jesus. We all know that he says that 'apart from me you can do nothing' (John 15:5). It's just that we too often live as if he had never said those words.

I've learned something new about being a fool for Christ too. An actor that I met suggested to me that the calling of the fool, particularly in Shakespeare's writings, is a calling of dignity and wisdom. The fool has a level of audience and friendship with the king that no one else has. He is able to express profound truth in the most simple, entertaining ways. He is a vital component in the royal court.

Called to be a fool? It's not so bad after all.

DECISIONS

DECISIONS, DECISIONS . . .

The prayer was straight to the point.

'Where have you gone, God?'

I punched a pillow, lay back on the hotel bed, and peered up hopefully at the off-white ceiling. I was drained by twenty hours of travel. The aeroplane food had been so bad I had considered praying for prophetic insight in order to identify it (*'I just sense that there's a chicken here with a bad back'*). Fellow passengers in crunched-together cattle class had been a challenge too. I recently sat next to a dear lady who decided mid-flight to begin breast-feeding her baby, a perfectly beautiful and natural procedure – but she did so without warning. As I lobbed another peanut down my throat, suddenly an Everest-sized breast appeared from nowhere. I cried out in terror, the baby cried out in terror, and I desperately started to pray for this unfortunate child who would surely grow up with an irrational fear of Switzerland.

Now jet-lagged and homesick, I focused again on that unyielding ceiling, half-hoping that its stark whiteness would roll back to reveal the colour and clamour of a vast, partying heavenly host. But the ceiling remained solid and clinical. There were only the beginning threads of a cobweb: no silken angel wings to be seen. I closed my eyes and listened with ears and heart: perhaps a comforting divine voice, audible or internal, would whisper reassurance and direction. But there was nothing, save the dull drone of traffic outside my window, the relentless dirge of domesticity.

'Where have you gone, God?'

Suddenly, the madness of my mission overwhelmed me. I had flown 6,000 miles to preach, with no clue as to what to say. No hint came from the organisers, ('just bring whatever the Lord gives you'). Fine! But right now, my hands were empty. Heaven was silent, and the absurdity, pretentiousness even, of a tiny being like me attempting to speak on behalf of the omnipotent creator of the universe crashed over me like a huge, suffocating wave, sweeping hope and confidence away in a second. Now I was bobbing and flailing around in doubt's icy dark waters.

My own words surprised and shocked me as I spoke them out towards the ceiling. 'Is this it then, Jesus? Are we through, you and I? After twenty-five years, is it all over between us? Where have you gone, God?'

Off white silence from above – outside, cars droned still.

Perhaps you've had a few chats with the ceiling over the years. Don't be surprised by those moments. Read the Psalms and you find the 'where are you, then, God?' prayer liberally scattered throughout. Maybe you occasionally wonder about the logic of living your life committed to the invisible.

Twenty minutes later, my hotel room still awaited angelic room service. Nothing happened at all, but for no earthly reason, I decided to continue my dance in the dark. Sometimes faith is a cold, hard choice. A decision to trust.

Cassie Bernall, a bright, seventeen-year-old Colorado schoolgirl, made that choice, not in the plush comfort and safety of a hotel room, but while staring down the barrel of a smoking gun. Cassie was quietly reading her Bible when 'Trenchcoat Mafia' members Eric Harris and Dylan Klebold marched in, armed to the teeth. Cassie was a relatively new believer, but was known on the campus of Columbine High School, Denver, as a radical witness for Jesus. One of the gunmen asked Cassie if she believed in God. The blood and the bodies around her made it clear what her fate would be if she owned up for Christ. Her response was calm. She decided. 'Yes, I believe in Jesus.' A second later a bullet took her to be with the Jesus that she loved so much. That night, her brother found a passage from Philippians that she had written out just two days before she chose to be a teenage martyr:

> Now I have given up on everything else
> I have found it to be the only way
> To really know Christ and to experience
> The mighty power that brought
> Him back to life again, and to find
> Out what it means to suffer and to
> Die with him. So, whatever it takes
> I will be one who lives in the fresh
> Newness of life of those who are
> Alive from the dead.

Eric Harris, one of the deranged killers, made a choice too. Seven days before the shooting, he was at a Christian coffee bar in Denver called 'Tuesday at Your Mother's'. A local band was playing, and the guitarist broke a string, which took thirty minutes to fix, so the lead singer used the unplanned pause to clearly present the Gospel. Then one of the band members had a word of knowledge that somebody present was going to kill someone or had just killed someone and asked for that person to come forward for prayer. No one did. Let no one ask where God was in the blood stained classrooms of Columbine High. He was right in the middle of it all, pleading and crying. But Eric Harris made a choice. Thirteen lives were snuffed out, before Eric and Dylan took their own lives.

Just twelve people attended the dark, tragic funeral of Eric Harris.

Cassie's Memorial Service was packed. The police, the district attorney, the world's press were all there to say goodbye to the girl who planted her feet, lifted her head and said, 'whatever it takes'. And seventy-five people made first time commitments to Christ.

Decisions, decisions . . .

THE BUNGEE JUMPER

The man has cobalt steel eyes, which mirror the deep blue of the rushing waters far, far below. He leans over the bridge for the ten-thousandth time, as if expecting to see something that he missed when, seconds ago, he last stared at the furious cauldron below.

Down there boils a swirling, rushing, watery chaos, oblivion waiting its time, waiting for him. The watching crowd are rigidly tense, afraid to move, wanting him to cancel his death-defying leap, yet at the same time desperate to see him finally clamber over the rail, and fly. Perhaps they feel guilty because their desire to see him jump is stronger than their hope for his safety.

The time has come at last. Checking the coiled cord one last time, he hauls himself up onto the narrow rail, arms outstretched: a portrait of balance and poise. He stands aloft, his cold eyes staring straight ahead. If his body is still, then his nervous system is somersaulting within him. He wrestles now with his brain, which screams its natural warnings about height and safety and death and, don't you know that humans aren't supposed to fly? His eyelids drop, and, head up still, he looks down. Now that he is on the rail, nothing stands between him and the abyss below. All that is needed now is the bending of his knees, pushing his whole body forward and out, into nothing: the jump itself.

His back is ramrod-straight still, every muscle taut, adrenaline screaming around his body at an impossible rate now. And then, casting all of his careful preparation to the wind, he breaks his concentration and turns his head to the breathless crowd. They are

164

transfixed. Smiling doesn't seem appropriate: it's too trivial. Their faces wear more serious expressions, grave, sombre even: sober tributes to his coming bravery.

The critical second arrives. The millisecond when you command your legs to push you out into nothing. Perhaps he senses the rushing onslaught of final fear, last second terror, and so, as if to flee the approaching paralysis that cannons towards him, he throws himself out, swallow-like, into the air. He glides outward, and then, as the crowds cry out, he plummets downward towards the boiling rocks and foam below. His stomach is in his throat, knowing now what it feels like to commit suicide. The wind rushes through his hair, as he plummets down forever. It is only two or three seconds, and then he feels the tension of the cord, straining against his weight to take up the slack. Let the calculations be correct, he should decelerate quickly, allowing him to just hit the rapids with his extended fists, before bouncing back up again, his graceful flight now rendered into a comical, clumsy elastic return. The bird becomes a man again, a helpless, bobbing, floppy doll, hurled up, and then down, up, and then down. He has beaten his fear, and dived into the face of death. The crowds far above cheer, voices from another world. He has done it. He is the bungee jumper.

What did it feel like, Jesus, the day that you peered over the parapet of heaven and prepared to take your own dive? Did you stare and recoil at the swirling madness below? Did the stench of hollow religion drift up and wrinkle your nostrils? You were to dive from that lofty, ordered, Father's house, down and down and down and still further down, into the murky morass of blood and pain so far below. You were to plummet from that calm and that place of song, into our sweaty, writhing chaos: from the world of rapture to our thunderdome of rape and rebellion; from immortality to the grime and tedium of time. Did you look around you at the sea of stunned angel faces, bowed and paled now at the sight of this holiest sacrifice? Was there any moment of farewell as you stepped, in a millisecond, from being the richest to being the poorest?

Our minds implode as we try to grasp the enormity of it all. But this mental feat is nothing, compared to the acrobatics that we experience as we think: incarnation.

Can we tiptoe for a moment onto that holy ground, and consider the magnificent Christ becoming a tiny, embryonic speck? What God-work could bring that metamorphosis about, as the Prince becomes . . . seed? This is a miracle, which dwarfs the five thousand fed by a long way. Perhaps this towers above the empty tomb, this longest journey ever, from throne to virgin womb. We have to blink, to look away, our eyes and hearts can't grasp this most enormous step.

No comforting cord held you in your dive earthward. It was the leap of no return, except by that one Calvary way. Down and down you came, and then the Creator-Partner of all this is becomes the pink-faced baby, crowned in a stinking shed. The angels couldn't resist – the magnificence of it all demanded that the heavens be split open for a while, if only to lonely shepherds on night shift. Wise men came by, drawn by reverberations in the spirit world, directed to the very spot by an obedient star.

'And little Lord Jesus, no crying he makes.' The writer of the otherwise beautiful carol got it wrong. Why wouldn't you cry? Like any baby, you felt cold, fear, damp, pain, and hunger. Who has travelled further: from the drawing board of creation, to a hay-strewn trough, from a king's robe to swaddling cloths?

And there was no cord wrapped around your ankle to spring you back to eternity's breast again: no way out, no emergency exit, just a cross, with its agony, and its ultimate reward.

You came, Jesus, and pitched your tent among us. Bold prophets and angelic messengers couldn't do what you did. Who has it all, and then throws it away? Where are the rich who have decided to walk the path of downward mobility?

But there is a truth that is a billion times more difficult to grasp than this incarnation of yours, which is hard enough to comprehend. My mind begins its own rebellion at the very idea of a throne to womb journey. But then, the *reason* for your voluntary dive is the news that really staggers. You stood on the handrail of heaven, and free fell . . . for us. You looked over, looked down, saw us . . . and jumped.

THE ITALIAN JOB

The man was cool. His singsong Italian accent skipped and danced down the telephone line, rich, exotic even.

'Jeeefffff, my deara friend, issa so good to 'ear your voice . . .'

I pictured the face behind this Latin accent that wriggled now in my ear. He would be wearing heavy black Ray-Ban sunglasses, whatever the weather, shielding dark, puppy dog eyes, and chiselled, handsome cheekbones, creased permanently either in a die-for-you smile or a furious don't-mess-with me scowl of fury. As for clothes, he would be a man in black: silk designer shirt, immaculate double-breasted jacket, trousers creased in vertical perfection. And he would be speaking to me via his mobile phone, a permanent appendage into which he would whisper, shout, cajole and convince from dawn till dusk.

His name is Gaetano Sottille; he is pure-bred Sicilian and he looks and sounds like a walk on part from *The Godfather*. But he is not in the Mafia – in fact, he was phoning me because of a little plan to give the Mafioso a slap in the face. Italy's answer to Billy Graham, Gae is a fiery Pentecostal evangelist, who believes that if it's worth preaching at all, it's worth preaching loud. With wild, flailing, windmill arms, and staccato bursts of oratory, he begs and commands his listeners to decide for Christ. He is a man obsessed: frantic to see 'soulsa saved', as he puts it. The name of his organisation proclaims his passion: 'Italia per Christo' (Italy for Christ). Utterly contemptuous of religion that fails to call the lost to the good news of grace, Gae travels the length and breadth of Italy, setting up makeshift platforms in city squares, bellowing the gospel to anyone who will listen.

But back to the Latin phone call. Gae was working on a very special project, hence his call to me. He was taking on the Mafia with a huge Christian demonstration. A year earlier, two court judges, including the famous Judge Falcone, had been blown to pieces by a mob-planted bomb on the road to Palermo airport, in Sicily. The world's newspapers had screamed banner headlines for a few days, but within weeks, the media had moved on, and the world had forgotten. But Gaetano had not forgotten. The first anniversary of the Palermo atrocity was not far off, so why not let the Mafia know that there were those in Italy who did not appreciate their bloodletting? The Mafia claimed to own Italy. Why not tell them that Jesus Christ is the only rightful King of the nations? The plan was simple. Gaetano put out a call to all believers in Southern Sicily. They were to converge upon Palermo by train, by boat, and by car, and hold a huge protest and proclamation meeting in the city square. They would carry signs that said, 'Down With the Mafia – Jesus is Alive!' And they would march through the city, accompanied by a couple of handy armoured cars manned by the police with machine guns at the ready, shouting defiance to the mob and praise to the Christ. And now, as Gae breathlessly poured his heart and strategy into the phone, I listened carefully, nervously.

Was he looking for reassurance and wanted prayer from his British brothers and sisters as he embarked on such a dangerous adventure? A satellite up-link from the UK perhaps, beamed directly into the square, to inspire and congratulate the brave crowd?

He didn't need reassurance, he assumed we would pray, and the word satellite was never used. He wanted me to go . . . in person. To march at his side, and to speak to the crowd. Visions of me waking up in the morning and staring into the eyes of a dead horse, kindly placed there by an Al Pacino look-alike, cascaded through my mind; the sights of a sniper's rifle as per

The Day of the Jackal; me walking through sweaty Palermo with a gigantic red and white target on my chest . . .

I am allergic to most forms of pain. I did not want to go to Palermo. God, surely, did not want me to go to Palermo. I told Gaetano so. It sounded lame of course, my stammering about needing to pray about it and not feeling right in my spirit etc. Phrases like these come in handy when needing a bit of divine endorsement for what we really want to do – or not do. Except with hard heads like Gaetano. He snorted, and then laughed. The matter was settled. I was going. 'All wooda be well', he said. 'God wooda be with us', he said. 'I wooda like a bullet-proof vest', I thought.

The march itself was a wonderful, carnival event: a celebration of the power of love that conquers hate and violence. There was the rumour of a death threat on Gaetano, which he met with humour as dark as his suit. As we walked together at the head of the march, he whispered words of comfort and encouragement in my ear.

'So, Jeff, ifa you notice a car pulling up beside us, with a beeeg gun steeking outa da window, feel very free to mention this to me . . . even if we are in the midst of veeeery important conversation.'

Delighted by his own wit, he slapped me on the back. I smiled, and wondered about how up to date my last will and testament was, and pondered the warm thought of a bullet searing and ripping its way through flesh – my flesh. I laughed at his dry wit: a shrill, high-pitched, terrified giggle.

Finally, we arrived at the city square, which was heaving with excited, sweaty believers, thrilled to be proclaiming their loyalty to the real boss. I took my turn with others who had flown in from around the world to bring their greetings to the exuberant crowd. The greetings went well, and a modern miracle was performed in that a dozen or so preachers managed to keep their comments to under sixty seconds each. Consider the temptation of a platform, a crowd, a television camera or two, and you'll know that the brevity of the preachers was a miracle something akin to the raising of Lazarus.

Two hours later, the event was all over – for me. But as Gaetano and I made our way through the rapidly dispersing crowd, I looked up at the windows of the apartments that overlooked Palermo city square. True Italian style, drying laundry left in the warmth of the late afternoon sun. Some of the Christians had draped banners out of their windows. They were like those 'no smoking' signs – you know the ones, a red circle with a diagonal line drawn through the picture of a cigarette. These banners had red circles too, but the diagonal line was drawn through the word 'Mafia' – and next to this blatant anti-mob symbol was written the word, 'Jesus'.

Within twenty fours hours, I would be gone from Sicily, a beautiful country with incredible food, fabulous scenery, and where judges are escorted home from the courts each day by the screaming sirens of an armed police patrol. I climbed onto a platform and took sixty seconds to be brave. I marched in a colourful line of believers for an hour, shouted for Jesus and then got a planc home, to safety, a million miles from Mafioso vengeance. But those who hung out their anti-mob laundry knew that they were making an irrevocable stand for Jesus. Their friends and neighbours would know that they were those Christians who stood up to the might of the terrifying network of international criminals, and declared Jesus is really Lord. Theirs were real decisions of courage.

FAITH

FLICK

It was one of those lazy late evenings. I sat sprawled on the sofa, television remote control in hand, flicking through what seemed to be a billion channels, but finding nothing of interest. I was even considering a visit to the shopping channel, so utterly desperate was I.

Flick. Extremely old episode of *Coronation Street* – Ena Sharples lives.

Flick. Australian gentleman in khaki shorts wrestling with an alligator.

Flick. Docu-soap covering the life of an Inland Revenue paying-in clerk.

Flick. Same Australian gentleman allowing a black widow spider to crawl up his leg, perilously close to disappearing up the aforementioned shorts.

Flick. A Christian programme. Well-known evangelist from across the pond. Suspect that he is wearing his present hairstyle because of a bet or a dare. Seated in a huge gilt chair, his ever-adoring wife sitting next to him, who appears to be breathlessly stunned at the wisdom of every comment he makes. Music, organ music I think, swirling softly in the background. A telephone number printed on-screen. A visa card symbol printed on screen as well. Hooray. God takes credit cards.

My remote flicking finger hesitated for a while.

'Just plant a financial seed into my ministry tonight, friend, and, I'm tellin' you, God is gonna bless that seed a hundredfold.'

He certainly looks dapper in that thousand-dollar suit. He reminds me of that slick con-preacher portrayed by Steve Martin in that uncomfortably accurate film *Leap of faith*. His deep blue eyes plead: he punctuates his appeal for cash with staccato quotations from biblical texts, most of them taken from the Old testament – and most of them taken totally out of context. The organ plays softly, hypnotically: a droning sedative. I imagine dear little old ladies putting aside the cat they were stroking and reaching for their handbags, some responding out of guilt: they wanted to put God first didn't they? 'Write a cheque.' Others would be getting stamps and envelopes out because they genuinely believed that they were helping the cause of the gospel by sending money to this man. 'Write a cheque.' And others would be buying into the 'fail-safe investment' approach – the blatant centrepiece of the evangelist's sales pitch. 'Write a cheque.'

Enough!

Flick. The Australian chap is looking very upset. The spider is exploring his shorts.

Flick. 'You see, my friends, God has raised me up as a ministry to stand in the gap for you and set you free from the financial, emotional, and spiritual chains that bind you. As you send the love-gift, as you pop that cheque in the post to me today, you enter into covenant agreement with me, and I will agree with you in prayer and *BREAK THOSE CHAINS* in your life in the name of Jesus . . .'

I'm very angry now, and I want to break his face. I punch the mute button on the remote, but continue to watch him, his hands extended in prayerful begging now, his wife dabbing tears from her perfectly made-up eyes.

Why am I so very angry? If this stuff helps and comforts people, then what's the big deal? I review my own feelings, as the evangelist continues to silently mouth his urgent message on screen. Some of it is the style, the slick hype that seems to grease the message. Some of my anger is due to the theology of his presentation, which seems to reduce a relationship with God down to nothing much more than a good deal, a formula for success, another way to dream the American dream. I am nervous of a gospel that is about principles, laws, and concepts. The gospel is not an invitation to take a series of steps. It's not even about 'four spiritual laws'. It's about the person of Jesus, and the call to take a walk with him. I also resent the suggestion that there are certain 'gurus' that God has raised up as intermediaries of prosperity and healing, who stand between God and his people – a new 'Charismatic priesthood'.

But now I am able to clearly see the reason for my anger. It is a rage birthed years earlier, in the early morning frost of an Oregon day. My anger was spawned as I stood, with a friend, in an onion field, of all places.

My onion farmer friend and I were close. He and his wife had shown us great kindness. We had spent many evenings around their kitchen table, talking about the Lord, about life, about our hope and dreams for the future. But my friend, partly through Christian television, partly through books and tapes, had become enamoured with the so-called, 'name it and claim it' teaching, and his family were suffering as a result of his flirtation. There is a well-worn adage: 'bad theology is certainly a harsh task master'. The truth of that adage was gouged into the faces of this family. The children had become ill, and Dad had initially refused to allow them to see a doctor, proclaiming that 'to consult with flesh and blood was a sign of unbelief'. The more obvious sign of this lack of flesh and blood consultation was the reality that one of the children nearly died. The doctor was finally called.

But the event seared most in my memory was the morning when, very early, the telephone rang, and it was my farmer friend. Would I be willing to go to the fields with him, to inspect his onion crop? He sounded very nervous, no up beat, jaunty faith-language now.

As I drove over to his house, I wondered why he would want me to go to the field – and began to dread the answer. I had heard that his crop was huge. It was due to be brought in any day – in fact, it was overdue – because of his 'faith'. He had taken some samples of the crop to a local fair, where they had won first prize – the onions were huge. This crop was worth hundreds of thousands of dollars, and was scheduled to pay his debts and feed his family for the year to come. But, instead of harvesting them immediately, and in response to 'a word from God', he had left them in the ground, claiming that the crop was to grow even larger before harvest. He scoffed at warnings from other farmers about the dangers of an early ground frost – that was 'unbelief', he said. His 'positive confession' was that the Lord was going to bless him with a crop that would be so massive, it would surely bear testimony to God's goodness and be a blessing to his own bank balance – which was seriously in the red.

Within an hour, I was to see the awful reality first hand. My friend had prayed, confessed, believed. But that morning the frost came and fatally bit the entire crop. He had heard the weather forecast, and now had to go to the fields to see if his fears were to be realised. We drove in silence, and walked out on what was now frozen wasteland. Tears filled his eyes, and mine, as he plucked one useless vegetable after another out of the stony earth. With a cry of anguish, he hurled one of the huge onions across the field. Everything was lost. Harvest time was over. Now he would have to pay someone to come and haul the useless crop away. Perhaps it could raise a few cents on the ton as pig feed.

There was a greater price to pay. The failed crop was the last straw for his wife. She filed for divorce: a Christian family was shattered. But there was more bitter irony to come.

Even this, according to my erstwhile friend, was the will of God for his life. The Lord was setting him free, releasing him from the encumbrance of a wife and family so that he could pursue the ministry that God had called him to. And the encumbrances wept when dad left home with a smile on his face and bold 'faith' in his heart.

I looked again at the face on the television screen. And I wanted to ask the grinning evangelist about my friend the onion farmer. But I know what he would say in reply. He would affirm that the farmer was guilty of presumption, not faith. He would tell me that one man's bad experience doesn't make truth any the less true. He would tell me that there are many television ministries that are faithful and full of integrity, and he'd be right. He would insist that it is wholly wrong and unjust to negatively characterise a Christian leader because he or she happens to be on television – and he would certainly be right there. He would tell me that God *does* want to be our provider and source. Correct again.

But I can never forget the day in the onion field. I remember the tears. I think of four children without a father, and of a woman who lies awake at night, restless, confused and battered by the knowledge that the man that she promised her life to – and who promised his life to her – now sees her as an encumbrance: a burden that Jesus has set him free from.

I punch the mute button again.

'So goodnight my friends, and God bless you all. My wife and I . . .'

Flick. The Australian gentleman has found the spider that had run into his shorts.

TURBO BIRDS

I don't like to admit it, but I was suffering from a nasty dose of cynicism. I had been wearied by the 'name it and claim it' antics of the American faith preachers, and bemused by the 'the Lord is so good, he gave me a parking space today' trivia. That's not to say that the God of the Universe couldn't spend his time searching for vehicular vacancies for his followers, should he feel so inclined, but it did seem that there might be more pressing matters clamouring for his immediate attention. One child dying of hunger every four seconds would be a worthy, alternative issue perhaps? But in rejecting the notion of the God-who-saves-us-from-the-parking-warden, I had come to the place where I refused to allow God to be involved in any of the minutiae of my life. When you think about it, for those of us who live in the third of the world's population where plenty is taken for granted, any kind of prayer request, except one involving a life or death situation, could be considered as unnecessary. I had lost sight of the Father in heaven who wants to be involved in the boring bits of even our relevantly affluent lives.

We wanted to move house. Whenever Christian leaders admit to wanting a bigger house, they usually excuse this ambition with the helpful disclaimer: 'Of course, we want a bigger house for the purposes of hospitality'. But we really did want a bigger house for the purposes of hospitality. Honest. Please believe me. We did. We also wanted a bigger house for the purposes of us, of course, but hospitality was high on the agenda.

We put our nice three bedroom terraced house on the market, and were underwhelmed by the response. For a whole twelve months it sat on the market, like a wallflower at a dance. During the year, two couples ambled by and took a look, but we had heard nothing more. And we had another problem – we couldn't find a house to buy anyway. The weekly scramble through the property section of the local newspaper had been in vain. We couldn't sell our house, and we couldn't find one to buy.

Reluctantly, we prayed. (Actually, the reluctance was mine. Kay has never been smitten with the idea that God is too busy to be interested in our housing arrangements.) We did not disappear to a wilderness and pray non-stop for forty day and forty nights. We did not fast. We didn't actually exert ourselves greatly, but rather, 'committed the issue to God' (mentioned it in passing when we were praying together one morning). The amen was said, and, as usual, nothing immediately happened. No angel with a housing speciality appeared before us to declare that, yeah verily, our supplications had been heard and a mansion was on the way. We just told God about it, and reminded him and ourselves as we did so, of the reality that he already knew anyway, and asked for his help. My expectations were low.

A couple of weeks later, we went to pick up our son, who was playing at a friend's house on the other side of the city. We parked our car at the end of the long, sweeping drive that prefaced the house, and waited for our son to come out. We had always admired this house whenever we had done the offspring collection run. We had never been inside, but, from a distance, it looked sedate, peaceful, and a long way beyond our budget. No sign of our son. I turned the car engine off, happy for the wait.

And then it happened. As we sat there, enjoying the fingers of late afternoon sunshine darting through the lush green trees, the singing began. The trees were crowded with birds, which were obviously having a profoundly happy day. Their song was loud and clear, a rich, chaotic symphony: loud and very clear. I commented on the sound.

'Kay, listen to those birds . . .'

Kay responded by saying that yes, she could hear the birds.

'Listen to that sound, listen to them singing . . .'

Kay, perhaps nervous that I was going to burst into a poetic moment, advised me that, yes, she had noted that the birds were singing, and that this was what birds occupied their time with. Singing is what birds do, she said.

'No . . . there's something about this . . . the way they're singing.'

My thoughts were interrupted by Richard clambering into the car. I started the car, and drove off. Perhaps Kay was wondering if I needed an application form for the RSPB. Perhaps she was wondering if I needed a little chat with a local psychiatrist. But I had heard the birds sing and, for some reason that I couldn't fathom for the life of me, there was something very, very important about that moment.

I forgot the bird concerto until a couple of weeks later, when we had a guest from America speaking at our church. Dale Gentry is a quiet, unassuming chap, who seems to have a rather uncanny ability to hear the faintest whispers from heaven. I had not met him personally, and he knew nothing about us, but he turned to Kay and me in a small meeting for leaders, and asked, with genuine interest, if there was an issue in our lives that we would like him to pray with us about. Yes, there was, I told him. We were trying to sell our house, and find a house to buy. Would he pray with us about that, please. He agreed.

He began speaking in the obligatory tongues for a few minutes, and then stopped, tapped me on the shoulder, and said something that I'll never forget.

'God is giving you a house, Jeff and Kay. I can see it in a vision right now; it's surrounded by trees. In fact, I can hear the birds singing in the trees . . .'

I smiled back at the man, and gave him my very best 'Yes I really believe what you are saying is true' look, but my heart immediately flooded with cynicism. He could hear the birds singing, he said. At that precise moment, I could hear a few birds singing as well, and they were all screaming 'cuckoo!' And then I remembered. I remembered the moment, weeks earlier, when we had sat outside the house that we had always admired, and heard the birds singing.

Dale continued. 'God is going to let you have that house . . . God says, "go get that house, go get that house".'

My mind swam again. Go get that house? Not only was the house way beyond our budget, but it wasn't for sale – a fairly significant detail. What was I supposed to do: drive over to the birdsong house, kick the door in, and say to the hapless owners, 'Get your furniture out – I've heard the birds'?

The meeting finished, and we drove home, thrilled and bewildered: knowing that God had spoken to us in a most remarkable and unusual way, but totally unable to process his word to any conclusion. The house wasn't for sale. What could we do? Nothing? Wait?

Perhaps it was another couple of weeks later when Kay received a telephone call. It was Richard's friend's mother – the lady who lived at the birdie house. She wanted Richard and her son, who were very close friends, to be able to get together urgently. She explained the reason for her haste.

'My husband has received a sudden and unexpected promotion. We are moving out of the area. I'd like our kids to be able to get together before we leave.'

Kay arranged for the junior get-together, and then proceeded to ask the very important question. Were they going to sell their house?

'Yes,' the lady said, 'of course.'

Had they listed the house with an estate agent?

No, they hadn't yet, the lady said, because the news of the promotion had only just come through. They were planning to put it on the market in a few days though.

Can we come and look at your house right now, Kay asked. I was listening to one half of the telephone conversation, and could hardly believe my ears.

'Yes,' the lady said, 'come on over right now.'

Go get that house, was the prophetic word. We chased over there, wishing we could have placed a flashing blue light on the roof of our car. Ten minutes later, we were inside the house, looking around the ground floor. Now we were in the garden. I was breathless with excitement.

'We would like to buy your house', I said.

'You haven't even been upstairs yet', they replied.

'Of course we need to look upstairs', I said, inwardly thinking, never mind upstairs, I've heard the birds sing.

Having dutifully examined the upper region of the house, we agreed a price and shook hands. But there was to be a condition to our deal. We would have to sell our house by the end of the week. They had to move quickly and, understandably, would have to put the house on the books of an estate agent if we had not sold our house by Friday, at 5 p.m. We marched down the driveway towards our car. 'We are going to sell our house by Friday at 5 p.m., even though its been on the market for a year', said Kay.

I looked up at the empty blue sky. 'Oh look – there's a pig coming in to land', I replied helpfully.

A couple of days later, our estate agent called. A man was interested in looking at our house. 'Send them over right away', we said.

We prayed urgently, desperately, frantically. As I showed the man around, I had to refrain from speaking in tongues or announcing, 'And this is the airing cupboard, *in Jesus' Name!*'

We got to the end of the tour. I asked the man what he thought of our house. I was very, very hopeful. He told me the house was very, very nice, and thanked me for showing him round, and left. I was ready to call the Samaritans, but couldn't find their number.

Two days to go before the birdie deadline. The next day, our estate agent called again: 'The man who came yesterday would like to look around again today, but bring his wife this time. Would this be convenient?' We replied that we felt sure that we could squeeze them in.

Another tour. Grunts of approval when we showed them the new bathroom. The hint of a smile, perhaps, when the new kitchen was displayed with pride? End of tour. Big question: what did they think of our house?

The couple told us, in stereo, that the house was very, very nice, and thanked us for showing them round, and left. I was ready to call the Samaritans again, but still couldn't find their number. I closed the front door behind them, a little too firmly, and announced to Kay that I had a vision myself – of dead birds falling out of the trees.

Why does God seem to enjoy last minute deadlines and only-by-the-skin-of-your-teeth answers to prayer.

Friday came – the last day – 5 p.m. deadline.

At 4 p.m., the telephone rang. I pounced on it. It was our friendly estate agent, who announced, very matter-of-factly, that the couple who had visited yesterday would like to buy our house, and had made an offer. I did my sums. The offer was not enough. 'It's not enough', I told the estate agent, who promised to pass the message on to the prospective buyers and get back to me when he had some news. I put the phone down, and looked at my watch. Fifty-five minutes to sell the house. The phone rang again, and the estate agent advised us that, yes, the couple definitely wanted our house and yes, they would pay the full asking price. I thanked the estate agent, advised Kay that I now had a vision of birds being resurrected, and proceeded to dance around the room. I phoned the birdie house, and told them we had sold, and the deal was on.

The next day, I spoke at an evangelistic event, and told the story that I've just told you. Six people made decisions to become followers of Jesus. One of them remarked, 'When you told that story about the birds, I knew that either there had to be a God – or else you were lying'.

We've lived in the house for four years now. I continue to be saddened by the 'Jesus wants you to be rich' approach to faith and prayer. But as I walk down the driveway each morning, I'm both thankful – and cautioned about a pendulum swing approach to the prosperity gospel, which robs God of the opportunity to be involved in the boring details of our lives. So, don't take this story as a recipe, a formula, or a pack-of-plenty strategy. Just know that God is interested, and able.

Hospitality means that we have a lot of people staying at our house. They often remark about how peaceful the place is – and how loud the birds are. Sometimes, the birds wake us before dawn with their colourful chorus.

Ours is the house with the turbo birds.

THE KEY RING

I looked across the sea of faces that made up the Sunday morning congregation. They were unusually attentive, some leaned forward, elbows on knees, hands cupped under their chins, apparently waiting for the next word. A young woman who sat on the front row quickly brushed aside another tear: I knew why. She had just given birth to her first child, and she had just been told that she had multiple sclerosis. During the pregnancy, the symptoms had mercifully lifted, but as her confinement ended, so the pain came again. Ten rows back sat an older lady, her face thinned out by the growing cancer within her. She was not expecting to live very long, and I had prayed with her just before the service started. Within days, she would be dead. Her eyes were clouded with the weariness of one who has lived and has had enough.

I was preaching that morning about pain, about the feelings that come to us when God seems a billion miles away – or not there at all. I had been very honest about my own Christian journey. God has been very kind to me; my life has been filled with his intervention and provision. One would think that doubt would never be a problem. But it is not so. There are the unexpected moments when, for a while, I wonder. Doubt sometimes pounces upon my shoulder for no discernible reason. I'm driving home after preaching at a service, perhaps one of those services that seemed to have been kissed by the kind presence of God. Perhaps there have been those who have decided to become followers of Jesus that night; others have been kind enough to tell me that their

187

lives have been strengthened because of what I have said, or that a book that I have written has helped them. I should be feeling encouraged and faith-filled, as I peer through the relentless wind-screen wipers and point the car homeward. But doubt does not just come to me when I observe great pain and suffering, the arbitrary scrawl of evil on the earth. Sometimes, it is in the aftermath of blessing that I feel this pressing in of the question mark in my head. What if there is no God? What if I have made a terrible wrong turn in my life journey. After all, I became a Christian when only seventeen years old: an impressionable age of naivety. Don't young people sign up for Marxism and then discover their enthused errors later in maturity? What if my conversion was just the result of an excited crowd, a convincing communicator, the peer pressure to believe, and the need to belong?

In my early days as a believer, I was not greatly troubled by nagging doubt. In fact, I remember feeling that I had all of the answers to the thorny questions of life sorted out quite nicely, thank you very much. Sickness and pain? Well, I sorted that nimbly by concluding (quite rightly) that we live in a fallen world and (quite disastrously) that sick people probably weren't exercising enough faith. It never occurred to me that my slick, slogan-based doctrines might bring great pain to someone for whom sickness was not just a theory to debate, but a daily reality to endure. The Second Coming? Easy! I knew the approximate time when Jesus was coming back, having purchased a chart from my local Christian bookstore. But years of study, reflection, and just the passing of life had led me away from my early certainties to a more agnostic approach to some issues that were previously part of my dogma. But sometimes my agnosticism could veer into momentary, mild atheism.

And so, that Sunday morning, I had told the congregation about my life night battles with belief. I had assured them that, if they themselves struggled, then they were normal human beings, not great sinners. The inability to fully understand, and the imperfect faith that results, is part of the human condition. Paul laments to his Corinthian friends that we see life but through a distorted lens. The great hope of the Christian is that one day we shall see clearly – with eyes that will focus on Jesus. In the meantime, we find ourselves on the dark side of the moon, with glimpses of the glorious God, but surrounded by the pervasive darkness and distraction that comes with life on earth.

And I had told them about a particularly difficult personal faith struggle, that had centred around the murder of young Sarah Payne, a bright, pretty eight-year-old, whose disappearance had captured the heart of the nation. Continuous media coverage, which included heartbreaking appeals from Sarah's parents and brothers and sisters, had touched a national nerve. Each day we hoped that she would be found, and as each day went by our hope was a little less that she was safe. Finally, the dreaded day came when the police announced that an unidentified body had been found: we all knew it was her. But it was the following day that really caught my attention. Some hitchhikers who had been in the area where Sarah was discovered came forward and said that they had heard the sounds of a little girl screaming in the night. Apparently, they had ignored the plaintive cries, thinking that some boisterous high jinks were the cause of the noise. The discovery of a body had changed their minds about all that. But it was their statement that cut into my heart like a dagger. *They heard the sound of a little girl screaming for help.* I replayed those words over and over in my mind, and searched for the cause of the anger that was boiling within me. And then I knew: I was angry with God. 'Didn't you hear the cries of a little girl in the woods, Lord?'

At one level, my anger was irrational. One child dies every four seconds because of hunger. God provides enough for all, but human greed is the killer. God did not orchestrate or organise the madness of Sarah's killer. But something snapped as I wrestled to understand why God did not come running through the dark, lonely woods.

It was compounded that night as I sat in a small Christian

meeting. It was one of those occasions for testimony and thanksgiving, a very real and genuine opportunity to share answers to prayer and give appreciation to the Lord for his care.

A lady had stood up to thank God for prayers answered regarding the weather. Apparently a school fete had been held locally, and so this lady had earnestly prayed for good weather: 'God, don't let it rain on the fete'. She went on to testify about how it had poured with rain on the Saturday of the fete – except on the fete itself. Apparently, there was a small area – the school site – that had remained totally dry. You drove to the event, and away from it, in pouring rain, but God had prevented the fete itself from getting wet. I smiled and nodded encouragement, but felt an overwhelming desire to stand up, scream the worst profanity I could think of, and ask why God had taken such care of the fete, yet allowed a little girl's screams to go unanswered in the woods.

I told the now rapt congregation this too, and I could feel a sense of relief sweeping over them, the release that comes when you discover that it's okay to wonder. And I told them about the Jesus who had so identified with the human condition of life on the dark side, that he had screamed, 'God! Where have you gone?' as he hung skewered to the cross. When Jesus sobbed out, 'My God, my God, why have you forsaken me?' it was a genuine question. Knowing, as we do, that this utterance was a fulfilment of prophecy, we can begin to think of his cry as some kind of script-reading as he nears the end. Jesus had neared the end of his life on earth with the question that is the hymn of the human condition: God, are you with us?

It was time to draw my sermon to a close. I had encouraged my listeners to be honest about their doubts: to be neither fearful nor paralysed by them. I had pointed to the Christ who came down in the very fullest heartbreak of what it can mean to live on this earth. And now, I wanted to call them to a new day, not of glib certainty or triumphalist hollowness, but to a quiet trust in the God who has been to the dark side and back. I started to use phrases like new dawning, new beginnings . . . and it was then that I heard the noise, coming from behind me, from the deserted platform. I couldn't identify either the sound or the source, but I had definitely heard a repetitive sound, and the congregation heard it too. They were nudging each other and pointing towards the platform, murmuring their speculations. I quickly asked them for silence, to just listen.

And there was the sound again, over and over – the sound of a cockerel crowing, 'cock-a-doodle-doo, cock-a-doodle-doo . . .' Repetitive, and crystal clear, the sound emanated from the platform that was empty except for the instruments and equipment that the worship team had deserted. I clambered onto the platform, and searched for the source. As I searched, the realisation of the incredible timing of this interruption hit me. I had been talking about a new day, a new dawning. Cue rooster, dead on time, to the very second. But where did the sound come from?

It was coming from a key ring, one of those novelty items that has an electronic alarm built in. One of the worship team owned this and always left it on the platform when she sat down to listen to the sermon. It had never performed before! I held the microphone down to the key ring, and the electronic rooster did its work, the noise reverberating now around the auditorium: 'cock-a-doodle-doo, cock-a-doodle-doo . . .'

I was embarrassed then, and I'm embarrassed now as I write this. A prophetic key ring. It sounds like the kind of madness that might be immortalised so humorously by my friend Adrian Plass. I had been offended by God's interest in the weather conditions for the local fete. Here I am, writing about him potentially setting off a key ring at just the right moment, in order to make a point, and in the very same chapter where I have spoken of issues of great depths of pain. The madness and potential superficiality of it all looms large.

So I gave the congregation a choice, and I give you the same choice now. I told them that if they wanted to believe that this little interruption was just a fantastic coincidence and nothing more, then that was just fine – and you, dear reader, may do the same. I also told them that if they wanted to conclude that perhaps the God who can use the foolish things of this world, in order to confound the wise, could speak through a key ring, then that was their choice too. It seemed to me that if he could speak through a donkey as he did to Balaam, then key rings weren't totally impossible for him either. But it was not, and is not, for me to force a conclusion on others that leans one way or the other. But I have a right to my own conclusion and, for what it's worth, I believe that God was involved in that mad moment.

But something happened to my faith that morning. I felt less able to understand God, and more able to trust him. I feel even more willing to not have all the slick answers. It's actually a relief.

But I still have the occasional panic, particularly during those boisterous worship times, when everybody else seems to be enjoying God-is-only-an-inch-away kind of worship, and I feel like I'm serenading the ceiling.

It's a good thing that God uses the foolish things of this world, like speaking donkeys, talking key rings, and me.

AVAILABILITY

STEP UP TO THE PLATE

I had flown to Salt Lake City to preach, and, for most of the journey, had pondered my sermon, and couldn't settle on the right theme. After sixteen hours' travel and much pondering, I was still quite sermonless. I arrived, found my hotel, and went to sleep with a heavy heart, vowing to wake early in the morning to rejoin the sermon safari and continue the hunt for the elusive talk. Five hours later the alarm clock screamed at me. I couldn't for the life of me work out where on earth I was in the world. It's tough to try to discern the word of the Lord when you can't even work out your precise geographical location.

I settled down to a jet-lagged prayer time, which is always dangerous, as one can never tell whether the thoughts that bounce around the weary walls of the mind are the whispers of the eternal God or the after-effects of aeroplane ravioli. Minutes later I began to feel that God was actually talking to me, but I wasn't too keen on what he was saying.

'Just go to the service this morning, and tell the people, "God says, 'step up to the plate'"'. The rest of the sermon will follow.'

Great! I've flown six thousand miles, endured food that bore a striking resemblance to an aerial view of a farmyard, and the congregation that have shelled out for this uncomfortable expedition are hoping that I will bring some teaching that is of high quality. What do I have to bring? One phrase: 'Step up to the plate', a term used in the game of baseball. I set off for the meeting with a heavy heart but a sense of faith that this could turn out

195

to be quite an adventure.

I was welcomed, literally, with open arms, and led into the prayer meeting. Dozens of people had forsaken the warmth of their beds that Sunday morning to come early to pray for the preacher and the worship team. And how they prayed: they were low on spit and high on inspiration. Some of them had just returned from some revival meetings in Florida, and were as high as the proverbial kite. They called on God for a mighty, Holy Spirit endued divine encounter that would shake the rafters. I stood there, the recipient of much laying on of hands, nodded my head and murmured my amens: all the time thinking about the epic body of teaching that I was carrying – 'step up to the plate'.

I'm ashamed to admit it – but I just couldn't bring myself to go through with what I now know was God's plan. I jettisoned the 'plate' idea, dismissing it as a by-product of too much time spent at 36,000 feet. I used a well-worn sermon, a tried and tested faithful old stand-by, and we had a *very* good service indeed: over a dozen people made commitments to Christ. Driving to the restaurant afterwards, I inwardly congratulated myself on dismissing the madness of the 'step up to the plate' plan. Why, God had blessed, people had become followers of Jesus: a sure vindication of my decision, right?

Wrong! Over lunch, I casually asked the minister what had been going on in the church of late. His response shook me rigid.

'Well Jeff, we've been concentrating on trying to encourage people in the church to realise that everybody has gifts that they can use as members of the body of Christ. Next week we begin a new sermon series that is designed to encourage everyone to make themselves available to God. There's quite a lot of excitement about this emphasis in the church.'

I wish I had never asked the next question, but something deep inside pushed me, already feeling that I knew the answer.

'So, what is the title of this upcoming sermon series?' I ventured.

'Oh, we're borrowing some baseball vocabulary. The series

has been publicised under the title, 'Step up to the plate'.

Oh, well done me! God had very kindly blessed my 'alternative service', but just think how much impact might have been made if, without any knowledge of the upcoming sermon series, I had just announced the word of the Lord and then followed the Holy Spirit through what would have surely been a huge response – and a very real strengthening of the faith of that church.

I placed my head in my hands and groaned. The minister thought that there was a problem with the food, until I explained – and apologised.

'Step up to the plate': what does it mean? Put simply, God was urging his people to make themselves available, to accept some responsibility, to play their part as members of his team. Generally speaking, the Lord uses people who want to be used: his preference is for willing volunteers rather than begrudging conscripts.

Isaiah is an example. Remember his call? The poor chap is having quite a crisis about his own naughtiness, and is intent on reciting his 'woe is me' speech endlessly. God sends an angel with a hot coal in his hand, with orders to burn Isaiah's mouth with said coal. This incendiary strategy was presumably designed to silence the 'I'm no good' speech. And then the Lord decides that there's a vacancy: a job must be filled. Now bear in mind, there's only God, Isaiah, and the odd asbestos-clad angel around, but God addresses Isaiah with what can only be described as a cosmic hint.

'Who will go, whom shall I send?' God asks.

Isaiah catches the heavenly hint, and offers himself for the task. He stepped up to the plate, and history was changed as a result. Meanwhile, back in the restaurant, I realised the irony of my mistake. Fear had paralysed me, and the result was that I had ceased to be available to the Holy Spirit for the delivery of his message. I had not *announced* the 'step up' message, and my refusal to articulate it meant that I was not prepared to actually *step up* myself.

I wonder how much of my frantic activity in 'ministry' comes under the category of my good ideas rather than the fulfilment of God's dreams.

God looks for availability, not ability. He's the Vine – we're the branches. Pray like this today: 'God, please help me to be a branch'.

God is looking for the next batsman or woman. Get the hint?

EXCUSES

Mrs Robinson was a bright, totally alive woman, who giggled uncontrollably whenever Jesus was mentioned: such was her infectious love for him. She was a lone parent, with two teenaged daughters. But she would soon be dead – the cancer in her a quiet, expanding labyrinth, uncoiling itself and spreading it's deadly venom every day – not long now.

I used to visit her every week, and she never failed to cheer me up. She told me her stories about her homeland, the West Indian island of St Vincent, and laughed at the thought of dying. This was no brave face, no denial. She knew that she was going to die, and she knew that Jesus had gone ahead of her. Her excitement about seeing him was palpable.

'No, Pastor, I'm not worried about dying, you see. But I am worried about my girls, Hazel and Denise. What will become of them? Oh Lord, oh Lord.'

And then her bright eyes would cloud over, and she would come back from heaven and land on earth again, real worry about her children causing her to rock back and forth, crying out to God.

'Oh Lord, oh Lord . . .'

And I would do my best to encourage her. 'Don't worry yourself now, Mrs Robinson, hasn't the Lord promised that if we cast our cares upon him, he would care for us?'

I would open my Bible and show her the scripture, 1 Peter 5:7. She knew it by heart, but would always look, as if checking to see that it was still there.

Week in, week out, she would laugh, and fret, and I would quote another scripture each time. One day I found a scripture that talked about God looking after the widow in her plight, and told Mrs Robinson that the Lord would make sure that Hazel and Denise were cared for. She seemed assured again.

As I came out of her house, God spoke to me, as he often does, by asking me an uncomfortable question.

'So then, how exactly am I going to take care of these children?'

I realised in a millisecond, that all of my praying flowery prayers and my quoting of Bible verses could be reduced to cliché if I didn't face the issue that God was raising. I considered the possibility that God was asking Kay and me to invite Hazel and Denise to be part of our family when their mother died. We had a young child of our own, and a very small house. This would mean disruption and inconvenience, and the 'how exactly am I going to take care of these children' question just wouldn't go away.

I decided to lay an impossible fleece before God. For those of you who are blessedly unfamiliar with this approach to guidance, it works like this: you ask God to fulfil a certain set of circumstances, and if those circumstances come to pass, then you agree that this will serve as a sign that God wants you to do something. It's a very useful strategy for those who are worried that God might be asking them to go to the mission field. You can ask for the impossible:

'Okay Lord, I will indeed go to Burma if, next Wednesday, when I am in the frozen food section of Sainsbury's, a Burmese soldier dressed as a leprechaun jumps out from the fish finger freezer chest, crying 'Okay then, begorrah. Come to Burma, and make it sharpish'. If the leprechaun is carrying a yellow bassoon and has wooden Dutch clogs on his feet, then I will take this as a sign of your call, and will head off for Burma immediately.'

I hit on the idea of a slightly more subdued, but equally impossible, fleece. I advised God that I was going to walk into our house and, without any discussion or prelude would simply announce to Kay that I felt that we should become foster parents to Hazel and Denise. The catch was that Kay was to say, without any deliberation or hesitation, 'sounds like a good idea to me'. Kay is a thoughtful, sensible person. Impulsive is not a word I would ever use to describe her.

I walked in to the house, pecked Kay on the cheek, and said 'I think we should foster Hazel and Denise'. Without a moment's pause, Kay gave her response. 'Sounds like a good idea to me.' And so we did.

Mrs Robinson died without any concern about the future for her children, and we became five. It was a wonderful time, although the neighbours surely wondered how we had managed to get two black children and one white. Perhaps there was something in the milk.

Don't get the picture of the Lucas extended family as something out of *The Little House on the Prairie*. It was a learning time for all of us, not least me. But Hazel and Denise became a very real part of our extended family.

I don't recommend the 'fleece' approach to guidance, although it works for some. But then again, I don't recommend clichés, pass-the-buck prayers, and making excuses for doing nothing either. Beware. God is about. He may just interrupt your life.

INFLUENCE

A+ FOR INFLUENCE

Influence is something we all have to a greater or lesser degree. We can use it every day. Often we are not aware of the affect that we have. A word here, a kind gesture there, a moment of time offered in the midst of a busy day. All of these can change a life, for good or ill, forever.

I will not name her – she would have wanted it that way – but she changed my life. She was the eternally harassed Religious Education teacher at a sprawling comprehensive school in Essex. Not many people were interested in RE. She knew this well, and seemed to be on a mission from God to change our indifference to interest. She was permanently in a rush. Years before the administrative stresses and pressures that came to the teaching profession with the advent of the national curriculum, she was seemingly on the go every second of the working day. She was also a head of year, which brought its own quantity of hassle. She could be seen running from classroom to classroom, with manic folders overstuffed with matters pending: arriving breathless, but smiling. Passionate about her subject, she spoke with intensity and conviction about God, as if her very life depended upon him. She would laugh and cry, encourage and cajole; her thin arms flailing around, her bony fingers stabbing and jabbing.

I heard that she was also a minister's wife, so, in addition to her pressure cooker existence at school, there was a whole other life with more than enough demands of its own. She convinced me that I should study RE to 'O' level. At the time I thought that all things religious (and especially Christian) were to be reserved for elderly people who needed to get out more. I wondered at just how 'useful' RE would be to my future career choice. But I took it any way, and passed well. She told me that I absolutely had to do RE at 'A' level. I wondered again about the academic usefulness of such a move. But there was something about her energy, about the sparkle in her eyes that could be seen so clearly when she spoke about her God. My friends thought that I was mad. What was I going to be when I left school, some kind of vicar? I joined in with their scoffing – mocked myself really. And I signed up.

Perhaps it was her patience that did it. Even insensitive students like us knew that other members of staff used to take advantage of her, use her, load her with work and expect her to smile and serve just because she was a Christian, and a minister's wife at that. I made my own contribution to the assault on her patience in the early years of GCE studies. During a lesson, when I gave the nod, every one in the class would simultaneously take a dive off of our chairs, and end up on our backs on the floor, arms and legs flapping wildly like stranded, demented sheep. She discovered that I was the architect and ringleader of the circus, and prescribed the ultimate punishment – I was to go to the headmaster's office and bring back the 'cane and book'. The thin bamboo cane was loathed and feared: its whip could raise a weal in a second. The black book was used to write the offender's name and details, a solemn testament to our misdeeds. I got to the door, genuinely afraid, and turned around and said, 'Please Miss . . . I'm really sorry . . .'

I expected a short rebuff and a reiterated command to fetch the instrument of torture, but instead, her face broke out into a soft smile. 'All right, Jeffrey. I forgive you. Now sit down and behave yourself.'

Amazed, I ran to my seat, and sat, attentive and tight-lipped, for the rest of the lesson. Never again would I be the conductor of the disruptive orchestra that was our class. I had tasted sheer grace.

She used to tell me about God, in front of the whole class. She wasn't at all subtle. 'Jeffrey. You need to be saved. Urgently', she would declare, and then came the smile again. In a way, I think I fell in love with her, but this was not the dizzy madness of a teenage infatuation, but a genuine admiration for someone who so obviously cared. I wanted to please her, to do well in my exams. I knew that the results were very important to her.

When I became interested in Christianity and made the decision to visit a church, it was her that I telephoned. She assured me that I would find a welcome at the little Pentecostal church that her husband led – and I certainly did. Her husband was everything that I hoped for. He wore a haircut of madness, with wild, frizzy hair, and his whole face was a broad smile. During his preaching, he would constantly tug at the plastic dog collar that constricted his neck, as if he was never completely comfortable wearing it. When I became a follower of Jesus, a few days after my first visit to their church, they both lavished love and kindness upon me. She was delighted, thrilled even, at my conversion. When I felt a call to ministry, she was the first person that I wanted to tell.

I lost touch with her for years. Ministry, and then a change of continent for us, and then a change of denomination, meant that our paths no longer crossed. And then came the day when I learned that she was dying. A terminal cancer was eating her life away, and quickly.

I went to see her. It was a slightly awkward meeting. I had changed denomination, and she didn't entirely approve. I felt like a little schoolboy again, as I had an audience with teacher, and feared a red correction mark or an 'F' on my paper. Her beautiful hair was gone; her head swathed in a turban to mask her baldness. I knew that it would be the last time that I would see her on earth. I wanted to thank her for changing my life. She smiled again, and told me how, twenty years after I left school, my school books were still in her possession: for some reason, a valuable souvenir to her.

I left, and a few weeks later, she left life. But her smile, her grace, her patience and her longsuffering made a deep and lasting impact on the wet cement that was my adolescent years.

I give her A+.

RED-LETTER DAYS

'It was a real red-letter day'. So the saying goes. Our days are many, and most of them are ignoble, without distinguishing features. They disappear from memory quickly. They were the black and white days: uneventful, uninteresting, and sometimes downright tedious. Nothing about them demands recollection: they fade fast into the blur of bland existence.

But there are also the bright, vivid days that stand out, that leap into memory's viewfinder – important days to be highlighted in red. These are the days of decision, which acted as rudders for our lives. New direction, opportunity and challenge came as a result of them. We recall them as milestones in our personal history, and wonder how our lives would have turned out if they had never dawned.

Sometimes, it is just a red-letter minute that changes everything. Pat Cook, a veteran missionary, and dear friend and hero of our family, recalls a day 'in the field' when she was out with colleagues driving on a well-worn route. On that particular day, she felt very strongly, and for no logical reason, that they should not take the usual road of their choice, but should go by a longer, alternative route. Minutes later they heard a distant explosion. A landmine had been placed right in the middle of the other road, instantly killing the occupants of the car that had triggered it. Pat's unsettled feeling had seemed little more than a hunch, but it was, in fact, a nudge from the Holy Spirit, and a red-letter minute, that saved her life and the lives of her colleagues. It was a decision that shaped her destiny.

And then there are the days of understanding – classroom days – where a significant lesson of life is learned. A nugget of that most precious gem, wisdom, becomes ours: an episode to be filed under 'unforgettable'. Some of these days are sunny, balmy, and bright: we feel happy enough to sing out loud. We slap our friends on the back and we toast the moments with the repeated question, 'Isn't this just great?'

Sometimes the learning days stand out in bold, dark red, because they dawned with dark, brooding skies and driving rain: days of pain and of mystery, where God was apparently nowhere to be found.

But be they happy or sad, they are our red-letter days. They are high, holy days. I think we should keep a list of them.

The day of your wedding, if you've had one, should be on this particular list. Pull out the album and laugh again at the fashions, the hairstyles, and ask, for the fiftieth time, 'Just who is that standing behind Auntie Hilda?' And as you remember, perhaps you'll recall again the pledges that you made before your gathered clan. Anniversaries should do far more than help Hallmark's shareholders: fond remembrances of the past can strengthen us for the present reality, and galvanise us for the future.

If there was a specific day in your life when you can remember making a clear decision to becoming a friend of Jesus, that should certainly appear on the list too. Others you might want to include might be:

That morning during the Sunday school class when the teacher explained how Jesus knew everybody, and still loved them. She pointed to you, just by way of illustration really, but you have never forgotten that pointed finger that broke the good news that heaven knows you – and loves you . . .

That stroll by the waves with the person who is now your partner. You kicked the mounds of sand, scattering great clouds of gritty mist; you screamed into the wind and chased each other around like ten-year-olds. You waved and swirled great trails of dripping, stinking seaweed around and, with laughing, shining eyes, peered at your future hopes and dreams together . . .

The moment that you realised that making a living is not the same as making a life. And that recognition was the dynamo that drove you to draw a thick black line through a few appointments. Refusing to be mastered by money or the deceptive security that comes from busyness, you refused the overtime, and maybe even turned the television off for a while so that you could enjoy the temporary giggling of your small children.

We've all got different criteria for deciding what makes a day a 'red-letter day', but I believe that we should remember, reflect, celebrate and rehearse our red-letter days to ourselves, and to our children.

Passover Day was red-letter in the chequered history of the Hebrews. It was the long-awaited moment when the powerful God danced into their jailhouse of Egyptian oppression, and brought angelic vengeance upon every household that hadn't decorated their doorposts with blood. The Hebrews would storm out of Egypt on an epic march towards a brighter future. Waves would stand up obediently to allow them to pass, and then crash down again to swallow up the so-strong army that pursued them. The Passover and the Exodus were ingrained as unforgettable memories into the very heart of Israel The vivid red ink of these days was designed to make sure that Israel would never forget that she was different, chosen, special. But even these vivid days were not enough. Like Cinderella with amnesia, she continuously lost track of her red-letter days, and in the forgetting, mislaid her own unique identity. And so, the painful covenant surgery of circumcision was given: a daily reminder to the Hebrew male about his identity and history. And still Israel forgets.

Don't be too quick to judge those hapless Hebrews. We all have a habit of forgetting what we should remember, and remembering what we should forget. So, will you permit me a red-letter reminiscence of my own? When I look back at the heady days of my first, faltering steps as a Christian, three red-letter days particularly stand out – although the first of them should be more accurately described as a red-letter fortnight . . .

As a brand new Christian, I was encouraged to attend a youth camp that was held on the green carpeted cliffs of Bembridge, on the Isle of Wight. My recollections of that two-week period include waking each morning with the delicious smell of sun-warmed canvas in the air; hazy afternoons of football and swimming; and then the breathless excitement of the evening chapel meetings, held in a huge marquee. Every evening was a date with God. We worshipped our hearts out, and then the preacher would speak. The speakers were called 'padres', and they were our heroes. They won our respect and friendship on the football field; seemed to remember our first names (even though there were nearly three hundred of us); said encouraging things when we prayed publicly and 'testified' in the meeting; or attempted to sing our hastily composed three-chord songs. They also had laughter lines on their faces, told funny stories with prowess that could shame some of the more proficient stand-up comedians of today, and clearly presented an unequivocal challenge and invitation to follow Jesus closely.

I loved camp, I loved sunshine, and I loved God with a heady mixture of passion and paranoia. I really wanted to be a hundred per cent proof Christian, and so my fledgling faith ignited both joy and grief within me in roughly equal measures. I was so desperate to get it right that I became almost obsessed, with my pursuit of the 'perfect' will of God. Our faith levels were often measured by the uncertainty of the emotional barometer: we *felt* led to do certain things and *felt* constrained to refrain from other actions. We *felt* that God was speaking to us and *felt* inspired to testify, pray, or whatever. The problem was that adolescence is not a glassy, flat millpond when it comes to feelings. I knew God loved me, hoped I loved him, and sometimes felt that neither was true. It was a confusing time – but God did meet me in the fog.

At the end of each meeting, there was the inevitable 'altar call': the invitation to walk to the front and kneel, either in quiet penitence or as a gesture of availability. I must have been the

preacher's dream, needing to respond to everything: the mingling
of ecstasy and guilt now a nightly cocktail. If an appeal had been
given for people to become French-speaking underwater basket
weavers for the gospel, I would have been first in line. My
favourite place was just to the left of the makeshift pulpit. My
knees wore that little spot on the grassy carpet thin night after
night. In those moments at the end of meetings, as the music
quietly played, and the hero-padres and others came and prayed
with us, lifelong decisions were made, tears of repentance were
shed, and vows were made that would stand the test of time. It
was a red-letter season, and one that I cherish.

Another red-letter day occurred just a few days after I became
a Christian. I was going out with a girl called Kay – now my wife
– who persuaded me that it would be a good idea to go away on a
church weekend. Great nervousness rushed over me as we hauled
our sleeping bags into the Christian conference centre. I was filled
with anticipation. Although I was only just a few days old as a
believer, I had been sensing that God was calling me to some kind
of ministry vocation – which seemed a mad consideration for a
brand new convert like me. The guest speaker was a most unusual
chap. Johnny Barr is a converted gypsy. He and his wife have had
more than their fair share of personal pain: having watched their
youngest son die in a car accident many years ago. Some of God's
choicest and most seasoned servants walk with the limp that
comes from a resolute march through life's rainstorms.

John was the guest speaker for our weekend – he did not know
any of us personally. Imagine our surprise, and consternation,
when he made a most unusual announcement during his opening
teaching session:

'God spoke to me while I was driving here today, and told me
that he has been calling three of you into some kind of leadership
ministry. In fact, the Lord told me your first and your last names.
This will not come as a surprise to you, but as a confirmation. I'll
be chatting with you more about this over the course of our
weekend together.'

I looked around the room, and wondered who these three special people might be. Despite the inner stirrings going on within, it just did not occur to me that John might have my name on his mind. There is something about the fallen human psyche that causes us to almost automatically count ourselves *out* when an announcement is made about God's calling and blessing – and count ourselves *in* when a notice is given about God's judgement. If John Barr had announced that God had provided him with the personal details of three great sinners who were between them guilty of great naughtiness, then I would have immediately assumed that he was talking about me – but an invitation to significance, calling, destiny? He had to be talking about somebody else. So, who might it be?

Twenty-four hours later, we were gathered for the evening meeting, when I suddenly became aware of God's power. It was like a force pressing down upon me, a gentle weight, a loving pressure. And I felt the need to speak out in tongues – something I had never done before. The pressure wouldn't go away. John was leading the meeting, and he stood up to make another announcement, so matter of factly.

'Someone here is being filled with the Holy Spirit, and is feeling the need to speak out in tongues. Just go ahead . . . trust God and speak now.'

I was caught between two emotions. On the one hand, I decided that I really didn't like this chap at all. He knew everything. God gave him the full names of those that he was working on, and now he was describing, without drama or hype, with a very matter-of-fact voice, exactly what was going on inside of me. Whatever next! What other personal and sensitive details might be revealed to this most unusual, somewhat strange man? Yet, on the other hand, my fear was mingled with faith. This was amazing: God was amazing; John was amazing. Still, I wrestled, anxious that I might make a fool out of myself. I didn't speak out in tongues – someone else did. The pressure lifted, and the meeting ended.

The final benediction was said, and I felt that I owed John an apology for not responding to his kind exhortation. I walked up to him, told him without introducing myself, that I was a new Christian who had allowed fear to paralyse me that evening. His eyes were warm with encouragement, and he exhorted me to quickly obey God the next time something like this happened. I turned to walk away, and as I did, he tapped me on the shoulder.

'Your name is Jeff Lucas, isn't it?'

I was gob-smacked, and at that precise moment, was unsure as to what my name was.

'Er . . . yes it is', I affirmed.

John's eyes were alive now, and he blurted out the breathless sentence that totally changed my life.

'God has been calling you into ministry, hasn't he? He told me your name, first and last, as a confirmation to you. Is this true?'

Of course it was true. I nodded, unable to speak at first, and then added, 'Yes, it's true.'

John snorted: 'Well get on with it then, son.'

And with that, he turned, and walked away. I went to my room and cried myself to sleep. God really did know my name. He really was calling me.

A few months later, I bumped into John Barr again, this time at a large Christian conference. I was delighted.

'Mr Barr . . . do you remember me? I've been looking for you.'

John paused and smiled his huge smile.

'No son, I've been looking for you.'

And right there, he laid hands upon me, and began to prophesy that I would have a preaching ministry that would be devastatingly effective for the kingdom of God; that I would be 'a hammer that breaks men's hearts'. It was another red-letter day.

At the youth camp, I wrestled and wept, and struggled to let God know that I was available. When I met John Barr, there was a sense of God imploding into my life, responding to my offer of availability.

Permit me a third day, a rainy day this time.

It was my much-anticipated graduation day after a couple of undistinguished years of study at a Bible College. I was no great scholar, mainly because of an impetuous, youthful impatience, and a hapless arrogance ('I don't need theology, I've got Jesus') which I now deeply regret. I scored zero in the Greek examination, mainly because I was playing table tennis while everyone else was struggling with ancient grammatical propositions. In fact, I wrote my name – in English – at the top of the Greek paper and then retired immediately to the table tennis room. I had a pious excuse for my sloppy study habits: I just wanted to get out into the real world and plant a church.

Graduation day signalled that we were now going to be let loose on the unsuspecting world. Look out planet earth, here we come! Kay was coming down to witness my graduation. We had a guest speaker flying in from Zimbabwe (then Rhodesia). Peter Griffiths was the leader of a mission compound that offered both a school and a medical clinic in the Vumba area. He was on his way to our college from the airport when the telephone rang in the principal's wood-panelled study.

It was Rhodesia calling, and the message was stark, ugly, tragic. The missionary colleagues that Griffiths had left behind had been attacked by some terrorists from Mozambique. All were dead except one lady, who had managed to crawl into the bushes. Within days, she too was to die in hospital. The women had been raped, and even the babies murdered too: skewered by rusty bayonets in turn. Now Griffiths was coming to speak, and he had no idea that his dear friends and fellow workers were dead or dying.

The awful news went around the campus like wildfire. The joy and anticipation of the day was replaced by a shocked, stunned silence. A student was dispatched to the front gate of the college, instructed to look out for Peter Griffiths' car. When he arrived, he was to be shown directly to the principal's study, where he would be told the awful tidings.

I will never know the details of the scene that unfolded in the study that day. I don't know if Griffiths was too shocked to respond, whether he cried, pounded the desk in rage, or just allowed his shoulders to shake with grief, his tears wet on the carpet. But I do know that he decided that the graduation ceremony must continue, and that he would have to keep his appointment with us as our commissioning speaker.

Our cheeks were wet with tears as he walked quietly to the platform. I can see him now, as he looked down into our bright, hopeful eyes, and his own bloodshot eyes seemed to be alive with grief and hope. His text for the sermon was, 'For to me, to live is Christ and to die is gain' (Phil 1:21).

He wept again as he told us about his beloved friends and colleagues, whose bodies were probably, even then, being transported to a mortuary far away in Rhodesia. And his eyes brightened once more, as he recalled their sacrifice, their determination not to budge from their calling and their laughter in the face of danger. And then he paused for a long time, looked into our eyes again, and asked us if we would be faithful to the Lord Jesus, whatever the cost.

Three years earlier we had begun our training, keen, brash and immature, feeling that we knew so much – why did we need this Bible school experience anyway?

Now, as we knelt to pray, we were sobered, but determined nonetheless. Griffiths himself has since died, and is now reunited with his missionary friends. But his was one sermon that I will never forget. It was a red-letter day.

A few years ago, I was speaking for a couple of days on the Isle of Wight. I had a light schedule, and a few hours to spare, and so I borrowed a bike, and rode across the island to Whitecliff Bay. I found the field where they used to pitch the marquee; I parked my bike, and managed to work out the whereabouts of that grassy little spot where I knelt years earlier. No tents there now, no makeshift pulpit, no slightly out-of-tune guitar music and no hero-padres to help me – just a big, lonely, very green field.

I knelt down on the spot that felt like mine. And I remembered. I remembered the sights and sounds, and smells, of those balmy days, lived two decades earlier. I wept sad and glad tears as I relived the joys and the anguished struggles of the past. And I talked to God.

I told him that a lot had changed in twenty years: that I was not the person who had knelt there years earlier; that my naive faith had gone forever; that I had seen Christians at their best and at their worst; I had seen gossip and immorality and hypocrisy. My naive, virginal faith was gone forever. But I told God that I still wanted to be his friend, and for him to be mine.

No orchestra played as I rose to my feet. No angel appeared and touched my uplifted head. But when I got up, grabbed the rusty old bike, and pedalled away, I knew that God had heard me, and that something very, very important had taken place. I had held a red-letter party, with just two invited guests, God and me.

Remember and celebrate the red-letter days. It's far more than weepy sentimentality – the remembering brings strength for the present, and hope for the future.